FORD DATA BOOK

FORDSON TO THE HUNDRED SERIES

Jeff Creighton

This edition first published in 1996 by MBI, an imprint of MBI
Publishing Company, Galtier Plaza, Suite 200, 380 Jackson Street,
St. Paul, MN 55101-3885 USA

MBI titles are also available at discounts in bulk quantity for industrial
or sales-promotional use. For details write to Special Sales Manager at
MBI Publishing Company, Galtier Plaza, Suite 200, 380 Jackson Street,
St. Paul, MN 55101-3885 USA.

ISBN 0-7603-0240-5

On the front cover: This early 1939 9N sports serial number 357.
Note the horizontal bars on the grille, the four-spoke steering wheel,
the small generator, smooth cast rear axle, and the snap-in battery
cover. *Chester Peterson*

On the back cover: A Model 9N. Note the aluminum grille. This was
later changed to steel in order to stand up against impact.
F. Hal Higgins Collection

Printed in the United States of America

Contents

ACKNOWLEDGMENTS

I am greatly indebted to Ford tractor collector and restorer Palmer Fossum of Northfield, Minnesota, for allowing me to conduct several hours worth of telephone interviews during the course of this project. His expertise is limitless concerning details of the Ford tractor. Also, I thank Marlo Remme of Dennison, Minnesota, for his assistance and phone interviews concerning the Fordson tractor. Who needs operators manuals when you've got a resource like Marlo?

Thanks to the following individuals for supplying manuals, sales brochures, literature, and photos: John Skarstad, head archivist of the Special Collections Department, Shields Library, University of California at Davis, for access to the F. Hal Higgins Collection and the wonderful 9N photos; to Clarence Goodburn of Medelia, Minnesota, for sales literature and hard to find advertisements; to Eldon Bryant of Fairfield, Iowa, for the same; to Gerard Rinaldi for allowing me to reprint aftermarket ads that appeared in his *9N, 2N, 8N Newsletter*. Special thanks also go to Wayne Wolfgram from the Corporate Trademark and Licensing Division of the Ford Motor Company for permission to reproduce sales brochure photos.

Special thanks to Stan Dammel of Odessa, Washington, for the photo reproduction work. As usual you were a lifesaver. Last, thanks to my editor, Lee Klancher.

INTRODUCTION

The Fordson and N-Series tractors are some of the most desirable collectable tractors. Their appearance is modest, their functions limited, but by the same token, they are as loved and respected as much as the Model T. The purpose of this book is to combine specifications, data, and short histories of the Ford and Fordson tractors from the Fordson (1917 to 1927 domestic model) to the 601-901 Series tractors. These were all-purpose machines designed for the small, one-tractor farm.

The *Ford Tractor Data Book* concentrates on identification of the various models, traces their advances and developments, and lists options, accessories, and aftermarket products. Specifications have been obtained from operators manuals, sale brochures, and other related literature. I have included both Ferguson and Dearborn implements with detailed specifications for each. This book is not intended to be used in place of owners or shop manuals, but to be used by the collector, restorer, or enthusiast for a quick reference. For this reason, serial numbers are also included. Some of the data, such as option and implement listings, are replicated in different chapters to eliminate flipping through pages to find that certain spring tooth harrow.

Unfortunately, much of the primary source material on Ford tractors, photos in particular, were lost while being transported from the old Tractor Division to the Ford World Headquarters some time ago. According to one source, the Henry Ford Museum also suffered an incalculable loss due to fire. Though much information remains at the Henry Ford Museum, especially company histories, this book should answer most Ford tractor lovers' questions. Luckily there are collectors around who are willing to share their knowledge on this subject; to them we should all be indebted.

CHAPTER 1

THE FORDSON

Henry Ford had been producing cars and trucks since the turn of the century, but he didn't begin experiments with the tractor until 1907. Many of his early prototypes looked more like stripped-down versions of the Model T than anything else, which was probably the reason why he referred to one of his first working model tractors as the "Automobile Plow." Initially, Ford had mounted the drivetrain on a conventional frame and continued to do so until the birth of the Fordson in 1916.

One of the earliest Fordsons used a Hercules four-cylinder engine, very similar to the Model T's engine only larger. Initially, the frame of the tractor was to be separate with all components attached to it. According to some sources, it was the design-engineer Eugene Farkas who suggested the use of the drivetrain itself for the frame. The design by Farkas consisted of a three-piece unit bolted together. Then, as the story goes, it was Ford who, on a visit to the foundry, suggested that the gearbox and rear axle sections be combined into one unit, reducing the sections from three to two. Not only was this the final design, but the use of the cast-iron unit frame would be replicated by virtually all other tractor manufacturers in the future.

Because Ford relied extensively on outside vendors, many of the components on the early Fordsons were supplied by various sources other than Ford. Besides the four-cylinder Hercules already mentioned, the worm drive was supplied by Cleveland, the gearbox by Timken, and the vaporizers by the Holly Brothers right outside of Dearborn,

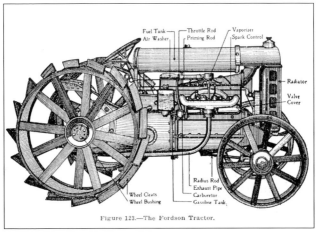

Figure 123.—The Fordson Tractor.

The line drawing above is the early model Fordson from the 1917 operators manual. Models prior to 1920 had 16 cleats and 12 spokes on each of the steel rear wheels. The radiator was the ladder type and the fuel tank was only one large chamber (mounted within the hood) with a two-quart gasoline starter tank mounted right behind the vaporizer and outside of the air washer. *Ford Operator's Manual, 1917*

Michigan. Many of these companies were later swallowed up by the Ford empire. Ford would eventually manufacture its own engine for the Fordson.

Early Fordson prototypes had the unenviable feature of worm gears that were mounted on top of the differential instead of underneath. The problem with this was that the seat for the driver was placed on top of the

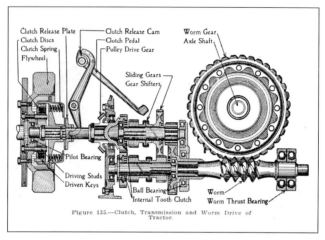

Figure 135.—Clutch, Transmission and Worm Drive of Tractor.

Diagram illustrating the clutch, transmission, and worm gear drive on the early Fordson. Pre-production "X" models were manufactured with the worm drive on top of the differential. Because so much heat was exchanged through the drivers seat, the final design had the drive below the differential as shown above. *Ford Publication, 1917*

differential, an area of extreme heat during operation that eventually found its way to the operator's posterior! The final design had the worm drive moved underneath where it could be adequately cooled in the oil bath.

The Fordson's more serious deficiency was that, in certain situations, it would flip over backwards. Implements at this time were hitched to the rear end of a tractor in the same manner that they were used with the horse. When a horse encountered a buried rock, it would stop. When the Fordson met with the same problem, it continued to gain traction with rearing or back-flipping being the end result. Ford tried to remedy the problem by offering optional rear winged fenders from 1922 on.

Another feature of the rear fenders was the tool and space compartments located at the bottom of each fender. Fenders for the Fordson could actually be found as early as 1920 from the Wiestel Company, among others. These fenders were a short version and did not include space for storage

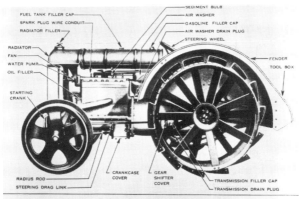

FUEL TANK FILLER CAP
SPARK PLUG WIRE CONDUIT
RADIATOR FILLER
RADIATOR
FAN
WATER PUMP
OIL FILLER
STARTING
CRANK
SEDIMENT BULB
AIR WASHER
GASOLINE FILLER CAP
AIR WASHER DRAIN PLUG
STEERING WHEEL
FENDER
TOOL BOX
RADIUS ROD
STEERING DRAG LINK
CRANKCASE
COVER
GEAR
SHIFTER
COVER
TRANSMISSION FILLER CAP
TRANSMISSION DRAIN PLUG

The Fordson Tractor—Oil Filler Side. Plate No. 3

Later model Fordsons like the one pictured above, went through a few changes. Cleats were reduced from 16 to 14 and spokes were increased from 12 to 14; the radiator was now solid instead of ladder (although for a while both types were produced), and the fuel tank was divided, combining both gas and kerosene tanks in one location. *Ford Brochure, 1928*

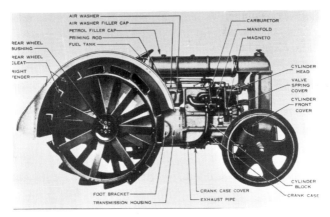

Right side view of the Fordson. Notice front wheel spokes. Later model Fordsons would utilize a thicker, wider five-spoke design as opposed to the earlier ten-spoke wheel. *Ford Brochure, 1917*

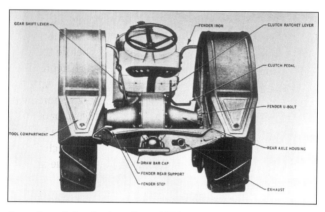

Rear view of the Fordson from 1928 operators manual. Note the "winged" fenders with tool and storage compartments. Earlier models had squared bottoms while the photo here shows the later "half-diamond" or "diamond point" version. These fenders were tapered to facilitate sharper turning with implements in tow. Note that the doors on compartments are triangular, while models produced before 1926 were squared. *Ford Operator's Manual, 1928*

and tools. The early "winged" fenders were squared at the bottom until 1926, at which time they were modified to a "half-diamond" or "diamond point" design that tapered the fender bottom to enable sharper turning when pulling an implement. The storage and tool doors also took on a triangular shape, as opposed to the earlier squared doors.

The Fordson was produced in the United States from 1917 to 1928, while production continued abroad until 1946. Few physical changes were seen on the Fordson throughout its United States production run. After 1919 the rear wheel spokes increased from 6 to 7 (12 to 14 inside and outside); cleats were reduced from 16 to 14; solid sides came about after 1919, replacing the ladder radiator sides; a divided fuel tank was implemented after 1920, doing away with the separate single two-quart gas starter tank; transmission brake and modified transmission bearings were later internal improvements. One other noticeable change was the increased holes in the drawbar from three to five.

Despite its reputation for back-flipping, more than 750,000 Fordsons were produced and sold in the United States between 1917 and 1928. In fact, just before the post-World War I slowdown in 1921, the Fordson represented nearly 50 percent of total tractor production in America. According to one source, in 1923 and 1925 more than "100,000 Fordson units were produced each year, or 60 to 75 percent of tractors produced by all companies." The Fordson would be the first lightweight mass-produced tractor of its kind, with the price eventually reduced to as little as $400 per machine.

Fordson Profile

The powerplant of the early model Fordson was very similar to the Ford car and truck engines, only a little larger. The driving force consisted of a four-cylinder Hercules, 4-inch bore and 5-inch stroke, 251.3-cubic-inch displacement that delivered 20 horsepower at 1,000 rpm. Later Fordson engines went through a few upgrades, such as a slight increase in bore and a displacement that rose from 251.3 cubic inches to 267 cubic inches. Horsepower was increased from 20 to 30. These later engines delivered 26 brake horsepower at 1,000 rpm and 67 pounds of compression when operating with kerosene; even better performance was achieved when using gasoline.

The majority of early Fordsons ran on kerosene that utilized several different vaporizer systems for fuel delivery. The earliest system was supplied by Holly Brothers. The first series of Holly vaporizers were used from 1917 to 1921. The company introduced an advanced model in 1922 that offered an attachment for the governor; the float bowl was also changed. In 1925, Holly came out with the Holly Hot Plate Vaporizer, designed primarily for burning kerosene. The Kingston vaporizer system was used from 1924 to 1926, offering two different types; one with the side-mounted carburetor, the other with a top-mounted carburetor. The top mounted system was designed mainly for gasoline-burning tractors. A carburetor adjustment lever was located on the dash.

Split view of engine from transmission with front view of engine, top left. Legend has it that Henry Ford himself thought of the two-piece casting. *Ford Brochure, 1917*

Early kerosene Fordsons were started with gasoline in order to warm up the manifold. Once the intake manifold was warm enough to properly vaporize the kerosene, the engine was switched over to burn kerosene. Early models had a 21-gallon fuel tank, which also served as the tractors hood, and a two-quart gas tank located on the right hand side of the tractor, next to the vaporizer and air washer (the divided fuel tank came out after 1920). The vaporizer was used to heat the kerosene vapor and then mix it properly with fresh air in order to obtain an adequate fuel mixture. The air supply was first drawn through an air washer that removed dust and grit before entering the system. The air washer also moistened the incoming air to reduce pre-ignition in the cylinders.

By 1926, competition from International Harvester prompted Ford to offer four different power options for the Fordson. These options consisted of (1) low-compression engine and low gear ratio transmission, (2) high-compression engine and standard ratio transmission, (3) high-compression engine and low gear ratio transmission (greatest power), and (4) low-compression kerosene-burning engine with standard ratio transmission. For belt work, only a high and low range was available. After 1925, gasoline became the standard fuel for the Fordson (instead of kerosene).

The transmission on the Fordson was a spur gear three-speed with one reverse gear. The constant mesh system was considered quite advanced for the era and went through only minor changes in later models. As mentioned earlier, the differential housed the worm gear reduction set that was to be modified before 1917, meaning it was situated under rather than on top of the differential. The clutch and steering gear were located in the rear of the crankcase housing; lubrication was furnished by splashing from the flywheel.

The Fordson's ignition system in 1917 consisted of a low-tension flywheel magneto and high-tension coils with a manual spark advance. Later models had a high-tension magneto with impulse coupling for automatic spark retarding, a feature that supposedly eliminated engine kick-back. On the dash was situated the spark lever that was moved in the up position to advance the spark and time of ignition.

Note: One way to identify a particular Fordson without the serial number is to look at the rear of the fuel tank. The earliest models displayed the manufacturer as "Henry Ford and Son, Dearborn, MI." After incorporation of the Ford Motor Company in 1920, the maker name read "Ford Motor Co., Detroit, MI." Finally, all Fordsons produced after 1927 carried the Irish label of "Cork, IR." Although this identification won't nail down a specific year, it will show the approximate time period of model years. The early U.S.-built Fordson was gray with red steel wheels.

Fordson Tractor Tests
Ohio State University, 1919

Test conditions...........................clay loam; soil, hard and dry; heavy subsoil

Rating..10-20

Rated engine speed.....................1,000 rpm

Engine...four-cylinder

Bore and stroke...........................4x5 inches

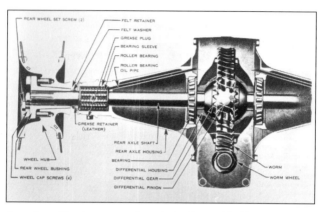

Rear view of Fordsons rear axle and wheel assembly. Note worm gear and wheel position. Roller bearings and leather grease retainers were used on both early and late model tractors. *Ford Brochure, 1917*

Type four-wheel

Wheel position ....in furrow
Weight..2,700 pounds/1,215 kg
Plowing speed ....3 miles per hour
Plows ....two 14-inch
Previous crop ....wheat
Footing ....good
Pounds of pull 1,304

Normal Test

Rate of Travel
Feet per minute............................272.5
Miles per hour 3.9
Horsepower...................................10.78
Depth plowed ....7.68 inches
Pounds of pull 1,687

Maximum Test

Rate of Travel
Feet per minute............................173.8
Miles per hour 1.97
Horsepower...................................8.88
Depth plowed ....8.25 inches

14

University of Nebraska, 1920
Test Number 18
Tractor rating ....18 horsepower
Rated engine speed.....................1,000 rpm
Engine ....four-cylinder
Bore and stroke...........................4x5 inches
Fuel ....kerosene
Tractor weight.............................2,710 pounds

Belt Tests
Rated load, two hours
Average horsepower...................18.16
Average rpm................................993
Gallon per hour (fuel) 2.48
Horsepower-hours per gallon.....7.32
Gallons per hour (water)............4.00
Temperature (air) 91ºF
Temperature (radiator) ....210 ºF

Maximum load, one hour
Horsepower 19.15
Rpm..   10.14
Gallons per hour (fuel)..............3.00
Horsepower-hours per gallon.....6.38
Gallons per hour (water)............3.35
Temperature (air) ....91 ºF
Temperature (radiator)...................209 ºF

Drawbar Tests
Rated load, 10 hours
Horsepower 6.06
Pounds of pull 886
Mph...2.57
Engine rpm 1,060
Percent wheel slip.......................28.80
Gear used ....Second
Lugs used....................................Angle
Fuel used ....Kerosene
Gallons per hour (fuel)..............2.48

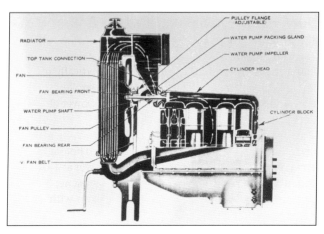

Side cutaway view of the Fordson engine from 1928 operators manual.

Horsepower hours per gallon.....2.45
Gallons per hour (water)............2.10

Temperature (air)............................ 89 ºF
Temperature (radiator)................... 209 ºF
Pounds of pull (maximum)........1,428
Mph..2.17
Total hours 34

Fordson Serial Numbers
1917 1
1918...255
1919...34422
1920...91712
1921..162667
1922..199448
1923..268433
1924..370331
1925..453341
1926..557509
1927..645611
1928..739583
1929..747584

1930...757265

Specifications*

Engine (1917-28): four-cylinder L-head vertically mounted length wise; 4x5-inch bore and stroke; 251.3 ci displacement; 20 horsepower at 1,000 rpm

Engine (1928-on): four-cylinder 4 1/8x5-inch bore and stroke; 267 ci displacement; 26 horsepower at 1,000 rpm; 67 pounds compression with kerosene; 30 horse power and 77 pounds compression with gasoline

Crankshaft: hardened and balanced

Pistons: lightweight diecast iron 5 1/16 inches long

Rings: 5/32 inches wide; one per piston

Main bearings: three main bearings; 2 inches in diameter and 3 inches long

Kerosene vaporizer (1917-28): Holly kerosene vaporizer

Kerosene vaporizer (1924-26): Kingston hot plate

Gasoline carburetor (1917-28): 1 1/4-inch Zenith down draft hot spot manifold

Valves: chrome silicon alloy steel

Cooling system (1917-27): Thermosyphon

Cooling system (1927-on): centrifugal pump, four-blade fan, 18 inches in diameter; tube radiator; 11-gallon capacity

Ignition system (1917-29): low-tension flywheel magneto with high-tension coils

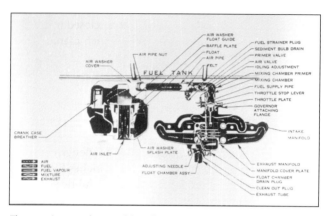

The vaporizer on a late model Fordson. Initially, two types of Holly Brothers vaporizers were used; the first series from 1917 to 1921 and the advanced beginning in 1922 that featured an attachment for the governor. Two styles of Kingston vaporizers were used from 1924 to 1926, one with a top-mounted carburetor, the other version had the carburetor mounted on the side. Both Holly Brothers and Kingston produced a "Hot Plate" model vaporizer that appeared on the Fordson between 1925 and 1927.

Ignition system (1929-on): high-tension magneto with impulse coupling; manual spark advance

Clutch: multiple-disc in oil

Transmission: three forward speeds and one reverse; constant mesh; internal gear clutch for each speed

Lubrication: splash lubrication

Fuel tank (1917-20): 21-gallon fuel tank over engine with 2-quart gasoline starter tank mounted on the right side of engine by air washer and vaporizer

Fuel tank (1920-27): 21-gallon divided tank over engine

Brakes (early): tractor was slowed by clutch depression

Brakes (later): multiple disc on transmission, 16 plates, operated by clutch pedal

Steering: Bevel pinion and gear sector enclosed in the clutch housing; four-spoke, 18-inch diameter padded steering wheel

Turning radius: 21 feet

Final drive: worm drive

Rear wheels: (prototype) 36 inches; (final design) steel 42x12 inches; 14 angle cleats 3 inches high; 7-inch extension rims (optional); lubricated from worm housing

Front wheels: cast-iron 30x5 inches; tapered roller bearings

Fenders: heavy-gauge steel; includes optional, available from Ford beginning in 1922, toolbox included

Weight (including fuel and water): 3,310 pounds

Wheelbase: 63 inches

Length: 113 1/4 inches with fenders; 102 inches without fenders

Specifications and data obtained from Fordson operators manuals and instruction books, 1917 to 1928.

Options

Fordson extension rims: for operating in sandy or loose soils; assembled on rear wheels with special clamps, making it unnecessary to drill special holes for mounting

Road bands: special steel bands that fit over the cleats on the rear wheels for travel over roadways

Fordson grouser plates: bolted to cleats on the rear wheels to add 3 inches to cleat depth; 14 plates to a set with nuts and bolts included

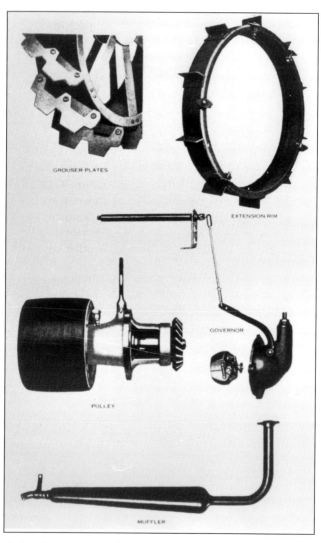

GROUSER PLATES

EXTENSION RIM

GOVERNOR

PULLEY

MUFFLER

Optional equipment, such as grouser plates, extension rims, belt pulleys and mufflers, could be had at extra cost. The above photo is from the 1928 operators manual.

Muffler: offered to those who required a quiet work area; cut down on exhaust

Belt pulley attachment: power pulley with or without shaft clutch; belt speed 2,480 feet per minute

Aftermarket Accessories

The Trackson Company of Milwaukee, Wisconsin, manufactured full-track systems (tracks circled front to rear wheels, no idler wheel) for the Fordson. The tracks were steel. The company also supplied its own steel wheels as part of the conversion kit. The Bell City Company made a track conversion kit also, furnishing four wheels, all the same size, with the full-track system. One other company, Hatfield-Penfield, offered a similar kit.

Numerous implement companies such as John Deere and Oliver built plows and a variety of tillage equipment for the Fordson. In many instances, the Ferguson mechanical hitch (a spring-loaded device) was used for raising and lowering implements.

CHAPTER 2

THE MODEL 9N AND 2N

While the Fordson was still being produced abroad in Cork and Dagenham, an all-new Ford tractor was being designed and would be used in tandem with Ferguson's three-point hitch. Harry Ferguson had tried his early Duplex Hitch with the Ford/Eros tractor, which was a conversion kit for the Model T and later in a venture with the Sherman Brothers that never got off the ground. For a brief period, Ferguson also joined with the David Brown Company (later Ferguson-Brown, Ltd.) and produced the "Black Tractor." Unfortunately, the lack of working capital, economic depression, and often dismal sales, seemed always to thwart widespread commercial success. After a falling-out with Brown in 1938, Ferguson met with Henry Ford at his Fair Lane Estate. This meeting led to the manufacture of one of the most popular small tractors in history, the Ford-Ferguson 9N.

It has often been debated whether the Ford tractor made the Ferguson System famous or vice-versa. Suffice it to say that both complemented each other and together proved that the small farm tractor could do the work of its larger siblings and be more efficient. Obviously Ford and Ferguson knew quite well that their "marriage" of convenience would not only usher in an era of efficiency, but also an era of agricultural firsts in small tractor technology. This era began in 1939 with the introduction of the Ford-Ferguson 9N.

Ferguson System

In simple terms, the Ferguson System incorporated the use of linkage (the three-point hitch) and hydraulics for implements being used behind the tractor. Five important factors of the Ferguson three-point hitch consisted of penetration without weight, automatic hydraulic control, traction without built-in weight, keeping the front end of the tractor down, and protecting the tractor and implement when an obstruction was encountered.

In an earlier time, the hitching of implements behind the tractor was similar to hitching them to a team of horses. Added weight was needed to keep an implement like the two-bottom plow down to a certain depth. With the use of hydraulics, added weight was no longer necessary. Another advantage to this type of system was its operation when encountering a hidden obstruction in the field. Hitting a buried rock with an implement powered by the horse wasn't that big of a problem because on impact the horse would simply stop dead in his tracks. As seen with the Fordson, fatal accidents could occur as the tractor, instead of coming to a stop like the horse, would continue to gather traction causing the tractor to rear. The nuance of the three-point hitch and hydraulics virtually eliminated these problems.

The Ferguson System also made it more practical to farm on uneven ground, thanks to hydraulic depth control. Implements were attached to the rear of the tractor by two bottom links and one top link. When the implement entered the ground, the bottom links began to pull while the top link started to compress or push, keeping the implement on a level plane while the tractor was in for-

The durable Model 9N in 1939 pulling a hay rake in Northern California. Notice the semi-horizontal grille with optional light kit installed. By 1941, the grille would be changed to the vertical bar type with a solid bar down the center. The solid bar was on the 1941 model only, being replaced by the slotted center bar the following year. The radiator cap was the hinged chrome type, later replaced with the black non-pressure type, then finally to the black pressurized type. Note: the 9N and 2N model tractors had six rear wheel lugs. The change to eight lugs centered on the wheel hub would come with the introduction of the 8N. The Ford logo on the 9N is mounted on top of the grille with the "Ferguson System" plate below. *F. Hal Higgins Collection*

ward motion. Not only did this top link help to press the plow into the ground, it also kept the front end of the tractor down. And what about getting bound up with that buried boulder? No problem. When this happened, oil was automatically released from the main hydraulic cylinder; the weight of the implement giving way to the tractor. Some of the weight was transferred to the front end of the tractor, keeping it firmly on the ground while reducing traction in the rear. The loss of traction not only prevented injuries, but also spared the tractor and implement as well.

The Ferguson System also aided in establishing the best possible traction depending on the type of soil being farmed. For instance, when plowing tight, heavy soils, the Ferguson-equipped 9N generated greater traction from the soil itself. The heavier the soil, the better the traction as the weight was converted to the traction needed. Conversely, working in light, soft soils created better flotation at the rear of the tractor, allowing the 9N to work in areas where heavier tractors couldn't without bogging down. The hydraulics for all operations consisted of a four-cylinder pump that supplied oil to the ram cylinder. The finger-tip control was positioned at the right of the operator for easy access and instant control of the implement. The Ferguson three-point hitch was also used on the 2N and later 8N tractors, even though Ferguson and Ford terminated their legendary handshake agreement in 1947.

Model 9N

Measuring only 115 inches from the front tire fin to the end of the lower link at the rear, the 9N was introduced in June 1939, just nine months after the Ford-Ferguson agreement. The powerplant, built at Ford's Highland Park factory, was the four-cylinder L head with a bore of 3.187 inches and stroke of 3.75 inches; displacement was 119.7 ci and the compression ratio was 6 to 1. The little four-cylinder generated 22 brake horsepower at 1,500 rpm and 28 brake horsepower at 2,000 rpm, with 84 foot-pounds of torque at 1,500 rpm.

Ford's experience with car and truck engines over the years was passed on to the tractor with the use of one-piece engine casting and removable cylinder liners. The cylinders, crankcase, and flywheel housing were all cast as one. To increase engine life and reduce cylinder wear, removable steel cylinder liners were used. When these liners became worn or damaged after years of service, they could easily be replaced, eliminating the costly process of reboring and honing. Removable cylinder sleeves had been in use since the 1920s, and it was crucial for Ford to incorporate this technology in order to compete.

Full-length water jackets were also used around each cylinder to ensure even expansion of the cylinders

Frontal view of the Ford-Ferguson 9N with extended wheels for row crop work. The tractor is either a 1939 or 1940 model as the grille is the semi-horizontal type with a solid center bar down the middle. Note the oval Ford logo with "Ferguson System" patch underneath.
F. Hal Higgins Collection

and for better circulation around the exhaust valves for increased cooling efficiency. These jackets extended all the way down to the crankcase.

The carburetor on the 9N was the plain tube, updraft type that was completely sealed against dust. A main jet adjustment was provided to change the fuel mixture under differing operating conditions. Fuel was carried (via gravity) to the carburetor from the steel fuel tank mounted within the engine hood. The tank held ten gallons, one gallon of that for reserve. Designers also included a sediment filter and clean-out (see Appendix for carburetors used).

Considered an innovation at the time was Ford's development of the oil bath air cleaner. All air entering the carburetor had to pass through the large oil bath. Also included as standard equipment was a precleaner (cartridge) that was designed to keep out excessive dust and chaff. The 9N used replaceable oil filter cartridges.

Another innovation on the 9N was the factory-installed reverse-flow muffler. This type of muffler not only directed the exhaust to the rear of the tractor, but also utilized expansion chambers rather than baffles in order to reduce back pressure.

The 9N electrical system was a welcome innovation considering the often lethal power associated with magneto ignitions found on the early Fordsons. The kickback felt through the hand crank alone could be quite intimidating. The 9N came equipped with a direct-drive distributor in unit with coil in a waterproof housing and a fully automatic spark advance. The generator was a six-volt with third brush control; the starter was the six-volt conventional automobile type. A safety starter switch mechanically interlocked with the gearshift.

The 9N was developed as a highly versatile all-purpose tractor to be used for assorted purposes on the small farm. Row-crop farming was one of these tasks. For this reason the Ford-Ferguson 9N was designed to change its wheel treads from 48 inches to 76 inches in 4-inch steps. The rear tread was widened by changing the position of the rims on the wheels while also changing or reversing the discs of the wheels. The front tread had holes at the center and the end sections of the front axle that would permit the axle ends to be extended up to 72 inches in 4-inch steps. Changing from 72 inches to 76 inches required reversing the front wheels so that the discs faced outward.

The 9N went through subtle changes between 1939 and 1942. For instance, the 1939 tractor contained an instrument panel that housed a starter button next to the ammeter, a key switch next to the oil pressure gauge, and a light indicating when the ignition was in the "on" position. Rear axle hubs were smooth on the 1939 model, front axle radius rods were the I-beam type, and front axle grease fittings were

Rear three-quarter view of the 9N with Ferguson three-point hitch and single bottom plow. *F. Hal Higgins Collection*

located on the forward side. The early radiator and fuel caps were the snap-on type instead of hinged. Cosmetically, the 1939 9N grille had nearly horizontal bars, while the steering box, grille, battery holder, instrument panel, transmission cover, and hood were made of cast-aluminum. Other notable characteristics to the 1939 model was the use of two crease bars on the rear fenders instead of just one, while the left and right brake pedals were identical as well as inter-changeable. The Ford logo appears on the top of the radiator with the "Ferguson System" plate attached underneath.

By the very next year, many changes could be found on the 9N for 1940: the three-brush generator and safety interlocked starter was introduced, while the hinged battery and fuel cap replaced the snap-on variety. In 1941, the 9N went through further changes consisting of a steel grille with vertical bars, a three-spoke steering wheel, differentiation between left and right brake ped-als, and the relocation of front axle grease fittings from front to rear for better protection. Further changes came about in 1942 when the 9N evolved into the 2N.

Model 2N

The 2N tractor was introduced in 1942 and was nearly identical to the 9N. In fact, according to some sources, the 2N evolved because of much needed improvements. Renowned Ford tractor collector Palmer Fossum remembered vividly one particular meeting he attended in 1941 with his father to discuss with Ford representatives the problems associated with the 9N. Suggestions were be solicited from the Ford people, prompting discussions about improved steering, brakes, a more potent electrical system, and radiator fans. As a result, Ford went about modifying and improving the tractor that eventually became the 2N.

New features introduced on the 2N were pressurized radiator, fitted grease nipple on the steering sector, an enlarged cooling fan with shroud, and reverse fan airflow (entering through the front of the radiator rather than from the engine side). The single-cast axle and hub

Model 9N with fully extended wheels pulling planter from the drawbar position. The drawbar in use appears to be the extended type offered as optional equipment. *F. Hal Higgins Collection*

Close-up rear view of the Model 9N operating with a row crop cultivator, attached directly to the hydraulic system and three-point hitch. Again the wheels are extended for row crop work. The cultivator followed the action of the front wheels of the tractor. With the aid of a marker attached to the front axle, the operator new exactly where to steer. *F. Hal Higgins Collection*

was also eliminated due to breakage under extreme working conditions. Other temporary changes were made out of necessity rather than for convenience. The war years took away industrial raw materials leaving the 2N, for a time, with steel wheels and a magneto (rather than battery) electrical system. By war's end, however, the 2N reverted back to what it was, with two final physical changes, the addition of sealed-beam headlights and a change in the radius rods to the tubular type.

The 9N/2N (as well as later N-Series tractors) could also be converted to run six- and eight-cylinder Ford Industrial engines. This particular option was made possible by Funk Aviation of Coffeyville, Kansas. Beginning in 1943, Funk had conversion kits for the Ford flathead six and from 1949 to 1950 for the V-8. (The Ford V-8 was rated at 100 horsepower.)The last conversion was for the valve-in-head straight six sometime after 1952. Depending on the powerplant desired, a partial list of the kit included a channel iron frame from the bell housing to the axle carrier; strap extension for the radius arm (to move the front end forward); a larger thick core radiator; a hood spacer; and an extension for the steering. Funk specifications for the six-cylinder engine are listed below, along with tractor tests, specifications, accessories, and the Ferguson implement line.

Why this 9N is parked in front of the Bank of America is not known. Whatever the reason, this is an excellent shot of the Ford product. Notice the tool box mounted just in front of the drivers leg. *F. Hal Higgins Collection*

Above is a Model 9N in the orchard. Even though Ford never produced an orchard version, you can plainly see how close the tractor could get. (Notice the wheels in their standard position. *F. Hal Higgins Collection*

Funk Six-Cylinder Conversion Kit

Engine: Ford Industrial six-cylinder; 3.3x4.4-inch bore and stroke; 226-ci piston displacement; compression ratio 6.7 to

1; speed rated continuous, 1,200 to 2,400 rpm.

Crankcase ....heavy-duty cast
Radiator ....30 quarts
Speeds.......................................1,200-2,400 rpm
Belt pulley .... 1,350 rpm
PTO... 545 rpm at 1,500 engine rpm
Height.......................................54.5 inches
Length ....78 inches
Weight......................................2,760 pounds
Capacities
Cooling system ....21 quarts
Optional fuel tank ....8.5 gallons
Crankcase ....8 quarts

Funk Six-Cylinder Conversion Parts List

Stack exhaust
Pipe, exhaust
Muffler, exhaust
Case
Plate, engine, rear
Ring, flywheel housing
Cover, timing gear
Brackets, transmission side (two)
Extensions, steering rod (two)
Pulley, generator
Generator bracket
Bendix drive, starter
Starter housing and bearing
Starter exchange armature
Solenoid starter clamp
Starter cable
Radiator
Upper and lower radiator hose
Hood

A Model 9N operating a post hole digger with hydraulics and PTO. *F. Hal Higgins Collection*

The belt-pulley assembly on the 9N was offered as an option. Notice the aluminum grille. This was later changed to steel in order to stand up against impact. According to some, the aluminum grilles could be dented just by brushing up against various high crops. *F. Hal Higgins Collection*

Governor housing and belt
Governor pulley and bracket
Carburetor and control choke
Rod, carburetor to governor
Tachometer drive
Rod, governor shaft to handlever
Governor cross-over shaft
Governor to shaft link
Governor support shaft lug
Two governor support straps, front and rear
Crankcase filler neck vent
Carburetor cap
Carburetor cap clamp
Carburetor to air cleaner tube

Fuel line, tank to pump; pump to carburetor
Oil line, engine to gauge

Ford-Ferguson 9N Tractor Test
University of Nebraska, 1940
Test #339
Rating ....12.68 horsepower
Rated engine speed ....1,400 rpm
Engine ....four-cylinder
Bore and stroke ....3 3/16x3 3/4 inches
Fuel...gasoline
Tractor weight ....3,375 pounds

Belt Tests
Test B: Maximum Load, Two Hours
Belt horsepower 23.56
Average engine rpm 2,000
Gallons per hour.......................2.434
Horsepower hours per gallon ...9.68
Pounds per horsepower hour ...0.623
Gallons per hour (water) 0.000
Temperature (radiator)..............183 ºF
Temperature (air).......................55 ºF

Test C: Operating Maximum Load, One Hour
Belt horsepower 23.07
Average engine rpm 2,001
Gallons per hour.......................2.368
Horsepower hours per gallon ...9.74
Pounds per horsepower gallon .0.619
Gallons per hour (water) 0.000
Temperature (radiator)..............179 ºF
Temperature (air).......................51 ºF

Test D: Rated Load, One Hour
Belt horsepower 20.24
Average engine rpm 1,996
Gallons per hour.......................2.130
Horsepower hours per gallon ...8.76

Another shot of the 9N in the orchard, this time with a spring tooth cultivator attached to the three-point hitch and Ferguson hydraulic system. Note the early four-spoke steering wheel. By 1941, the four-spoke unit would be replaced by a three-spoke version. *F. Hal Higgins Collection*

Pounds per horsepower hour ...0.688
Gallons per hour (water) 0.000
Temperature (radiator) ....171 °F
Temperature (air) ....51 °F

Test E: Varying Load, Two Hours
Maximum rpm during test 2172
Minimum rpm during test 962
Weight of tractor as tested ....3,375 pounds

Test F: Maximum Load, Drawbar
Drawbar horsepower 16.31

Drawbar pull pounds 2,146
Tractor speed...........................2.85 miles per hour
Percent slippage 13.55

Test G: Operating Maximum Load, Drawbar

Rated gear...................................first
Drawbar horsepower...............12.61
Drawbar pull pounds 2,236
Tractor speed ....2.11 miles per hour
Percent slippage 17.33
Rated gear...................................second
Drawbar horsepower...............15.92
Drawbar pull pounds 2,101
Tractor speed ....2.84 miles per hour
Percent slippage 14.46
Rated gear...................................third
Drawbar horsepower...............17.02
Drawbar pull pounds 872
Tractor speed ....7.32 miles per hour
Percent slippage 4.45

Test H: Rated Load, Drawbar

Rated gear...................................second
Drawbar horsepower...............12.80
Drawbar pull pounds 1,568
Tractor speed ....3.06 miles per hour
Average engine rpm 1,399
Percent slippage 6.70
Gallons per hour (fuel) 1.610
Horsepower hours per gallon ...7.95
Pounds per horsepower hour ...0.758
Gallons per hour (water) 0.000
Temperature (radiator)..............178 ºF
Temperature (air)......................60 ºF

Serial Numbers for Model 9N
(Serial and motor numbers are incorporated on left-hand side of the engine block)
1939..1

1940...10234
1941...45976
1942...89888
1943...105412

Serial Numbers for Model 2N*

(Serial and motor numbers incorporated on left-hand side of engine block)

1942...99003
1943...105375
1944...126358
1945...169982
1946...198731
1947...258504

Note that serial numbers for the 9N/2N over-lap for a two-year period. This was due to the over-supply and distribution of parts still in stock for the 9N product.

Model 9N/2N Specifications

Engine: four-cylinder L-head; 3.187x3.75-inch bore and troke; piston displacement 120 ci; compression ratio 6:1

Horsepower: 23.87 maximum belt horsepower; 20.29 rated belt horsepower (85 percent of maximum); drawbar two 14-inch plow capacity with Ferguson hydraulically operated implements; maximum drawbar without Ferguson hydraulic system of control, 16.90 horsepower; rated drawbar horsepower (75 percent of maximum), 12.68 horsepower

Governor: variable speed, mechanically operated centrifugal type, governor regulation from 400 to 2,000 rpm

Standard tire sizes for the Model 9N were 4x19 for the front and 10x28 for the rear. Rear tread widths could be adjusted from 48 to 76 inches in 4-inch steps (rear rims needed to be reversed); front wheel width could be extended up to 72 inches in 4-inch steps, with an additional 4 inches of width by turning the wheel discs outward. *F. Hal Higgins Collection*

Lubrication: gear pump supplies direct pressure oiling to crankshaft, camshaft, and connecting rod bearings; crankcase capacity 6 U.S. quarts

Oil filter: replaceable cartridge type

Ignition: direct-driven distributor in unit with coil in waterproof housing, fully automatic spark advance

Above is the 9N demonstrating its turning radius, which was up to eight feet when using the brakes. The tractor is in the middle of row crop work with all four wheels extended. A row crop cultivator is being used and is in the raised position. *F. Hal Higgins Collection*

Generator: 6-volt with third brush control

Starter: 6-volt conventional automobile starter with safety starter switch interlocked with gearshift lever

Battery: 6-volt, 85 ampere-hour capacity; 13 high plates

Cooling system: pump with circulation of water through tube and fin radiator; pressurized system; fan, six-blade, 16-inch belt-driven; prelubricated bearings; system capacity, 12 U.S. quarts

Fuel supply: welded steel tank carried within hood; capacity, 10 U.S. gallons; use of a two-way valve on the sediment bulb allows 1 gallon to be held in reserve

Air cleaner: oil bath with dust receptacle for easy cleaning

Carburetor: updraft, plain tube

Muffler: reverse-flow type

Clutch: 9-inch single dry plate; clutch plate pressure increased by centrifugal force as engine speed is increased

Transmission: sliding gear, three speeds forward and one reverse; shafts mounted on roller bearings

Final drive: spiral bevel gear drive with straddle-mounted pinion 6.66 to 1 ratio; four pinion differential mounted on tapered roller bearings; semi-floating drive axle with integral axle shafts and wheel hubs mounted on tapered wheel bearings

Steering: bevel pinion and twin bevel sectors controlling both front wheels independently; tread of front axle adjustable without disturbing any steering connections; rubber-covered steel steering wheel 18-inch diameter

Power take-off shaft: for Ford-Ferguson equipment, extends from rear of axle housing, 1.125-inch spline; shaft speed of 545 rpm at engine speed of 1,500 rpm

Hydraulic implement control: four-cylinder pump supplies oil under pressure to the ram cylinder; valve has automatic and manual control; control lever is located at the operator's right for instant control of the implement

Another view of the 9N during plowing operations. The plow is down to its proper depth and is maintained by the Ferguson system of hydraulics and three-point hitch. The "system" maintained proper depth regardless of uneven ground conditions or variations of soil thickness. *F. Hal Higgins Collection*

Brakes: 14x2-inch internal expanding, two shoe, fully energizing type; one simple accessible adjustment on each brake; brakes operate independently on each rear wheel and are controlled by separate pedals to facilitate short turning

Wheels: front-steel disc fitted with 4x19 single-rib pneumatic tires on drop center rim, 26 pounds of tire pressure; rear-steel disc fitted with 10x28 traction tread pneumatic tires on drop center rim (8x32 early model), 12 pounds tire pressure

Drawbar: adjustable type; included as standard equipment

Dimensions: tractor wheelbase, 70 inches

Normal tread—front 48 inches, rear 52 inches

Front tread—adjustable by means of
extending axle ends and reversing front
wheel discs to 76 inches in
4-inch steps
Rear tread—adjustable by means
of reversible wheel discs and reversible tire
rims to 76 inches in 4-inch steps
Overall length—front tire fin to end of
lower link,
115 inches
Overall width—64 inches
Overall height—52 inches
Ground clearance—13 inches under center, 21
inches under axles
Turning circle—16-foot diameter with
use of brakes

Weight: 2,340 pounds (no liquid in tires)

Color: dark forest gray

Selected Parts Specifications*

Valve, valve lifter, and timing specifications

Valve head diameter:

Intake ....1.537 inches

Exhaust.....................................1.280 inches

Angle of seat..............................45 degrees

Diameter of valve stem ....0.3105 to 0.3115 inches

Diameter of valve stem end......0.548 inches

Clearance setting.......................0.0125 to 0.0135 inches

Valve lifter diameter..................0.9994 to 0.9996-inch

Valve timing (cold at .0100 to .0115 clearance)

Intake opens...................................6 degrees before top center

Intake closes.................................22 degrees after bottom center

Exhaust opens...............................38 degrees before top center

Exhaust closes ....6 degrees after top center

43

Connecting Rod Specifications

Weight, rod with cap ....580 grams
Diameter of bearing ....2.0935 to
                                      2.0945 inches
Length of bearing......................1.120 to 1.130 inches
Diameter of piston pin bushing .7503 to .7506 inches
Length of piston pin bushing...1.34 inches

Piston, Pin, and Ring Specifications

Weight of piston.........................360 grams
With pin and rings....................482 grams
Piston pin diameter................... .750 inches
Width of compression ring....... .092 inches
Width of oil control ring ....0.155 inches

Camshaft Specifications

Camshaft bearing diameter.......1.7965 to 1.7970 inches
Bearing length
Front ....1.54 inches
Center..1.48 inches
Rear ....1.48 inches

Crankshaft and Main Bearing Specifications

Weight of crankshaft.................41 pounds
Diameter of journals ....2.25 inches
Diameter of crank pins ....2.1 inches

Length of main bearings

Front ....1.6 inches
Center ....1.66 inches
Rear..1.6 inches
Diameter of main bearings ....2.25 inches
Specification data obtained from Model 9N operator's manual and sales literature, 1941.

Options

Belt pulley: carried by self-contained drive unit,
         quickly attach able to rear of the tractor.
         Pulley diameter, 9 inches; width, 6.5

The earliest Model 9N's came with cast-aluminum hoods and grilles because stamping equipment for steel was not ready in time for production. Fortunately steel came not soon enough as the aluminum components were extremely fragile. Above is a close-up of the left-hand side of the 9N. This early "9" has the original I-Beam radius rod and no freeze plug, making it almost certain that it is an original 1939 model. *F. Hal Higgins Collection*

inches; speed, 1,352 rpm; belt speed, 3,190 feet per minute at 2,000 rpm engine speed; pulley gear ratio to power take-off shaft, 1.86. Rotates in either direction

ASAE Power take-off adapter with safety shield: self-contained drive unit that is quickly attachable. Has standard ASAE spline shaft, 1.375 inches; shaft speed of 545 rpm at 1,500 rpm engine speed; engine to shaft ratio, 2.75 to 1

Lighting kit: includes two headlamps and a taillamp with license bracket, switch, and all necessary wiring

Storm cover: designed specifically for the Ford tractor with Ferguson system. Protects against dust, dirt, and water

Steel extension wheels for the Ford N-Series tractors. R.S. Horner of Geneva, Ohio, offered these extension wheels for use on golf courses, in parks, and for work in rice fields. R.S. Horner manufactured the Horner Universal Wheel. *Don Horner Collection*

Air cleaner extension: for extremely dusty areas, screen and bowl that is attached above the tractor hood

Half cab: accessories available from Ford Motor Company's tractor and implement division for 9N through 900 Series tractors. Features of the cabs included folding tops, rear drop curtains, doors, engine compartment flaps, and tilting windshield. Made of weatherproof canvas on a metal frame

Aftermarket Accessories

•Both the ARPS Corporation of New Holstein, Wisconsin, and the Canadian Bombardier Company offered track conversions for the N-Series tractors. The tracks were used primarily for operation in snow, marshy land, and soft ground. Oddly enough, the Bombardier system was derived from the company's own snowmobile design. The tracks gave the tractor added traction and maneuverability similar to four-wheel drive. Tracks were positioned around the rear wheels; an idler arm running from the tractor's differential supported the idler wheel that picked up the front portion of the track: though Bombardier tracks were made primarily for the Ferguson tractors and the ARPS for the Ford Ns, either company's tracks could be used for each tractor. ARPS offered three different tracks : regular duty, heavy-duty, and extra heavy-duty. Various attachments were also available.

•The Tokheim Oil Tank and Pump Company of Fort Wayne, Indiana, produced an all-weather cab for the Ford-Ferguson and Ford N-Series tractors. The all-steel cab was easily installed by one man. The cab itself was an insulated one-piece cab with all-steel turret top and corner posts and outfitted with adjustable windshield, door, and rear curtain.

•KR Wilson Company of Buffalo, New York, supplied a tractor dolly with built-in jacks for the Ford tractor. Wilson was well known to the Ford Motor Company, as it already supplied factory-approved tools and equipment for Ford, Mercury, and Lincoln passenger cars. The dolly was designed to roll underneath and raise the tractor without the use of a conventional jack. Drivetrain units could be moved along the dolly independently with the use of a screw-operated slide that ran upon the dolly's frame. Hold-down straps were also supplied to keep units tightly in place while being serviced.

•Not so much an everyday aftermarket accessory for the average farmer was the Gledhill Road Machinery Company's use of the Ford Tractor to power its Convertible Road Roller. Gledhill Company literature stated that, "in a few minutes time it can be converted into a rubber tired tractor or back again to a road roller," giving its owner the benefit of two machines for the price of one. The roller was steered by the standard steering mechanism of the Ford tractor. The Road Roller came with a 3-ton roller with 600-pound water capacity in front rolls and a combination ballast tank and roof with 3,500-pound capacity totaling 5 tons! Rear rolls were also available, being installed in place of the rubber tires. Apparently the little Ford tractor had no trouble moving all that weight around. The Gledhill firm of Galion, Ohio, also made motor graders and shapers powered by Ford tractors.

Common Ferguson Implements

Moldboard plow: Connected to rear of the tractor by the three-point hitch. Coulter discs are heat-treated high-carbon steel; jointer blades are heat-treated alloy steel; 13-inch diameter pressed steel disc wheel is mounted on rear landside. Two-base plow is 21 inches from share points to beams; single-base plow is 22 1/2 inches from share point to beam. Plowing depth is controlled by the hydraulic system.

ROAD ROLLER

NEW, PRACTICAL, FAST, 3 TO 5 TON ROLLER ALL IN ONE

The New Gledhill Road Roller with Ballast Tank and Roof—5 Ton as Illustrated

Highway and construction men have always wanted a compact, practical roller—a roller that was fast, dependable and at the same time economical. The NEW Gledhill Roller has these features and many more.

Powered with the new Ford Tractor, this roller is so designed that in a few minutes time it can be converted into a rubber tired tractor or back again to a road roller, thus giving you the advantage of two pieces of equipment at the price of one, and in addition the choice of two weight capacities. The roller weighs three tons and with a unique Gledhill development can be increased to five-ton capacity. This extra weight is added by simply filling the front rolls with water which adds 600 pounds. If additional weight is desired, 3400 pounds of water can be added to the combination ballast water tank and roof, making a weight of five tons. The combination tank and roof is 9' 6" long, 6' wide and 12" deep and is equipped with ballast baffle plates which make it practical when the tank is not completely filled, by avoiding and holding the water from splashing from one end or side to the other.

Another interesting conversion with the N-Series is the Gledhill Road Roller. The front axle was completely removed from the Ford tractor and rear wheels were replaced with rollers. The tractor may be a 9N/2N, mainly because of the rear six-lug configuration and hub that was typical of that time. *Don Horner Collection*

Disc plow: Frame is a bolted construction of high carbon steel; discs are 26 inches in diameter. Disc scraperswere furnished for sticky soils and to control furrow pitch in terracing. Two tapered roller bearings are for discs and the furrow wheel. Maximum plowing depth is 12 inches.

Middlebuster: Clearance is 19 inches from point of base to beam (11 inches when implement is raised for transport). Row width adjustments are from 36 inches to 42 inches in 2-inch steps. Coulters were supplied as an accessory.

Disc harrow: Heavy steel and angle bar construction with discs constructed of heat-treated high-carbon steel. Hard maple wood bushings are 5 inches long and boiled in oil (the are replaceable). There is a shield for keeping out dirt and grit. The angle of gangs could be set on the angle selector rack from the tractor seat; straightening or repositioning of the gangs could be accomplished by using the hydraulic fingertip control without stopping.

Bush and bog harrow: There were two types: Model 820 (lift-type) and Model 823 (pull-type), with scrapers, discs, and gang carriers. Model 820 was attached to the three-point hitch, while the Model 823 was connected with the drawbar to the lower links.

Spring tooth harrow: This was constructed of high-strength steel in two sections. It is controlled by a ratchet-type control lever for each section, regulating depth and angle of teeth. There are 17 teeth for maximum resiliency and tension. The width of cut is roughly 6 inches.

The Tokheim Company was one of several companies that manufactured all-weather cabs like the one pictured here. *Bill Hossfield Collection*

Subsurface tiller: The tiller is mounted on middlebuster frame (not included) and attached to the three-point hitch; it can be operated manually or automatically (Ferguson hydraulics). There are three high-carbon steel sweeps 4 inches wide with a 24-inch spread across the back wings. The width of cut is 5 feet, 6 inches. Rolling coulters (three) were 16 inches in diameter.

Tiller: Mounted directly to the three-point hitch and controlled by fingertip hydraulic control, its working depth is maintained automatically. Individual spring tine release avoids breakage. Tines were constructed of heat-treated alloy steel for deep tillage. Numerous types of sweeps and shovels were available for the Ferguson tiller: reversible points, quack grass points, chisel points, alfalfa points duckfoot points, and crucible spear points.

Weeder: It is connected to the hitch and hydraulics. Width was 13 feet 4 inches; cultivates four rows of corn and similar crops; six to eight rows of beans and other like crops. Seventy-four high-carbon spring steel teeth supplied adequate soil agitation and penetration.

Agricultural mower: Steel constructed with cutter bar lengths of 5, 6, or 7 feet. Came with a wood pitman 59 3/8 inches long to provide a smaller angle at the cutter bar to reduce friction and wear and is connected to the hydraulic lift. The cutter bar runs off of this pulley drive from the PTO. A heavy-duty model was also available.

Sweeprake: For front-end work. It has I-beam frame construction supported by steel to give added strength. Push-off teeth were constructed of wood, gathering teeth were steel. The sweeprake's lifting arms were connected to the hydraulic arms of the Ferguson system. Load capacity of the sweeprake was 600 pounds.

Feed grinder: Operated by tractor belt pulley, the all-purpose grinder would grind any feed ensilage, roughage, corn, or grain. The grinder had both a dry grind side and a wet-inch grind side for raw material. It could be run on as little as 7 1/2 horsepower. A variety of knives, screens, and grinding hammers were available.

Loader and crane: Made by Baldwin, the loader and crane could be operated in cooperation with the Ferguson system on the Ford tractor. Both loader and crane were front-mounted. The capacity of the bucket loader was 10 cubic feet, with a maximum lifting height of more than 8 feet. Rated capacity for the crane was 1,500 pounds. Baldwin also manufactured an oil heater that attached to the tractor's exhaust pipe to generate heat during cold weather. The heater kept a better flow of oil to the raising ram cylinders.

Cordwood saw: This was operated with the belt pulley attachment and Ferguson hydraulic system. It was used primarily for cutting raw cordwood. The unit could be transported easily from one location to another. Standard blade was 30 inches, although 18-inch and inch blades were available. It had a solid steel frame. The saw speed was 1,200 rpm.

CHAPTER 3

THE MODEL 8N

The 9N/2N tractor soon evolved into the 8N that was unveiled in July 1947. Numerous improvements followed, making the 8N one of the most popular N-Series tractors ever. The year 1947 signaled the end of the Ford-Ferguson handshake agreement. With the death of Henry Ford in 1945, grandson Henry Ford ll took control of the company and in doing so broke off the relationship with Harry Ferguson, a decision that was actually made in 1946. It had been widely held by Ford management that Ferguson enjoyed a great deal to benefit from the 1938 agreement than did Ford. The Ford people generally assumed more financial risk at the tractor end of the business, while Ferguson controlled both tractor and implement prices through the dealer network. The profits of servicing the former and the latter also fell to Ferguson.

With the relationship terminated in late 1947, Ford announced not only the production of the 8N but also a completely new line of implements (Dearborn). Ferguson went on to produce the 8N look-alike TO-20, and later the TO-30, before merging with Massey-Harris in the mid-1950s. Initially the Ferguson "system" remained on the 8N for its production run, prompting Ferguson to file a $340 million lawsuit for patent infringements and other damages relating to loss of business. After six long years of litigation, Ferguson was awarded close to $10 million in 1952. Throughout the course of the courtroom struggles, Ford did manage to alter the 8N with respect to patent violations and in 1953 designed a hydraulic system of its own.

From the front cover of the sales brochure, "Power for Production" comes the Model 8N. Introduced in 1947, one of the noticeable differences in the 8N from the 9N/2N is the change in lugs from six to eight on the rear wheels. The lugs are also more centered on the hub. Another addition was the scripted logo on the sides of the hood and on the inside of the rear fenders. Noticeably absent is the Ferguson System patch displayed under the Ford oval, even though the tractor still utilized the same Ferguson hydraulics. Ford's new hydraulic system would have to wait until the introduction of the Golden Jubilee in 1953. Ford also introduced its own Dearborn line of implements; the Ferguson line was no longer used, nor promoted, by Ford. *Ford Brochure, 1951*

8N Profile

One of the numerous improvements to the 8N was to the engine. The same four-cylinder L-head that was used with the bore increased fractionally from 3.187 to 3.188 inches; piston displacement remained at 119.7 cubic inches, with an advance in compression ratio from 6:1 to 6.50:1. Torque as well was increased from 84 foot-pounds at 1,500 rpm to 92 foot pounds at 1,500 rpm. Company literature states that the maximum drawbar horsepower in second gear was 23.16; rated drawbar horsepower in second gear (75 percent maximum) was 17.37; maximum belt horsepower at 2,000 rpm was 27.32; rated belt horsepower (85 percent of maximum) was 23.22. The rated speeds were 1,500, 1,750, and 2,000 rpm respectively. The pistons in the 8N were aluminum, a change from the cast-steel pistons of the earlier 9N; the pins remained full floating.

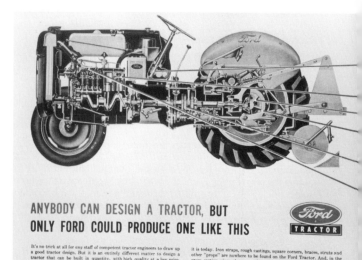

A cutaway view of the 8N from the 1951 catalog. The 8N was powered by the four-cylinder "L" head engine and constant mesh four-speed transmission. Note the script on the inside of the right fender.

The ignition system that came a bit later on in the 8N consisted of a side-mounted distributor with a separate coil, replacing the older integral unit just underneath the fan. The drive was by the spiral gear off the camshaft. The cooling system on the 8N was quite similar to earlier N-Series tractors with the exception of a four-blade fan instead of the six-blade blower type. The suction fan could be had at extra cost, operating like the standard automobile fan, taking air in from the front of the radiator. The steering on the 8N consisted of the ball-nut gear automotive type, an improvement over the old bevel pinion/twin bevel sector gear. Ford literature claimed that with the new setup, "two and one-quarter turns of the 18-inch steering wheel will turn front wheels through their entire range of travel when tread is 48-inch." The entire unit operated in oil for longer life.

One of the most welcome improvements on the 8N was the use of the four-speed transmission. Still using the constant mesh, the four-speed aided greatly in versatility around the farm. First and second gear basically remained the same, while third became a good cultivating gear and fourth the road gear. Traveling in fourth gear at 2,000 rpm, the 8N could reach 13.64 mph, as opposed to 11.75 mph at 2,200 rpm with the three-speed.

Two different hydraulic controls were used on the 8N, the first of which was the Constant Draft Control (an original Ferguson feature), the second being the Implement Position Control. With the Constant Draft Control, the desired depth for subsoiling or discing could be achieved by lowering the implement with the tractor's hydraulic Touch Control. Once set, the hydraulics would keep a constant depth whether working stiff or uneven ground. The Implement Position Control lever ensured that a constant depth would be maintained in varying soils. The system was activated by raising the lever to the up position located at the right of the driver's seat.

The Proof-Meter (tachometer) was another addition to the 8N, and Ford made it very clear in its sales brochures that Ford was the only tractor company that

ALL THIS IS STANDARD EQUIPMENT
AT THE FORD TRACTOR'S LOW PRICE

SAFETY STARTER
Six-volt push button type. Unless the tractor is in neutral this starter will not operate. No danger of starting the motor in gear and jamming the tractor's radiator into the end of the shed.

POWER TAKE-OFF
Operates power take-off driven rear attached and side mounted mowers, post hole digger, sprayers and dusters. Can be easily converted to drive A.S.A.E. standard power take-off driven implements.

STANDARD DRAWBAR
Eleven holes in bar permit you to get correct line of draft. Clevis bracket used for attaching swinging drawbar and implements that are not designed to hitch to tractor linkage.

AIR CLEANER
This is the heavy-duty, time-tested oil bath type. Screened air intake is easily removed for cleaning. This cleaner with proper maintenance attention will do much to lengthen engine life.

OIL FILTER
Here is another "insurance policy" that's standard equipment to help you keep all moving engine parts to their original close tolerances. This filter has a large-capacity cartridge are easy to replace.

BATTERY
In the Ford Tractor this is not an "extra." You get plenty of capacity; 13 plates, 6-volt, 80 ampere hour type. Remarkably easy to check and service . . . just raise the screen panel on the hood.

WHEEL SPACING
You get 4-wheel stability and the ease and accuracy of steering that only 4 wheels can give. You also have a range of wheel spacing to fit just about any row crop that's grown. Front and rear wheels can be spaced in four-inch steps from 48 to 76 inches! Wheels on one side can be set wide while wheels on the opposite side are set narrow—a valuable feature for harrowing and hillside work.

This ad shows standard features such as safety starter, the large capacity oil filter with replaceable cartridges, PTO, and 11-hole drawbar. The far right of the photo shows the wheel spacing of the 8N. Rear tires were 10x28 (standard) and could be adjusted from 48 inches to 76 inches in 4-inch steps. Front tires are 4.00x19 and also could be adjusted from 48 to 76 inches. *Ford Brochure, 1951*

ADVANTAGES OF FORD TRACTOR **POWER**
ON THE INTENSIVE 1-TRACTOR FARM

The intensive farm operator seldom has many big jobs—but he has an almost endless number of small jobs. Since his manpower is usually limited, he must have sufficient tractor power to make his man-hours count. His tractor must be "nimble" so that he can get around in tight spots, up close to fences, work the corners of odd-shaped fields. His object is to make all his soil contribute to his prosperity.

Adequate Power For All Jobs

The Ford Tractor does not have the handicaps of a "garden" tractor—it's a full 2-plow tractor and has ample power for the intensive farmer.

If it becomes desirable to rent, lease or work a few extra acres on shares, you have in the Ford Tractor sufficient power to make these ventures profitable. Also, with the Ford Tractor, custom work is open to you as a profitable sideline. With implements carried "up" you can speed to your customer's place and back home in jig time. They'll like the work you do for them.

Lets You Jump From One Job to Another Fast

The Ford Tractor's triple quick-attaching of implements is perhaps a more pronounced advantage on intensive farms than on other farms since as many as three or four changes may be made in one day. Think of the tractor and man-hours this feature alone provides!

"Nimble"—Fast Moving

To work in the "tight" places you just can't match the Ford Tractor. First of all it's short-coupled and Dearborn Implements are close-attached. Then you have automotive-type steering, improved brakes and hydraulic control of implements. All this helps you to intensely work more land for more profit—for greater prosperity.

The Model 8N was extremely popular as a two-plow tractor, and was used for a variety of row crop tasks. The photo above shows the 8N with front and rear wheels adjusted fully, pulling a Dearborn manufactured rigid-shank cultivator. *Ford Brochure, 1951*

had it. The new meter actually had five functions indicating engine revolutions per minute, tractor ground speed in forward gears, PTO speed, pulley speed, and operating hours. The hours of operation reading was an accurate means of determining when the tractor should be lubricated. The PTO speed reading gave speeds both for load and no-load rpm; the pulley speed module told the operator where to set the throttle for operating belt-driven machines.

Other new features were cosmetic. For the first time, the Ford logo appeared in red script on the side of the hood just behind the nose up front and on the inside of both rear fenders. The castings were also painted red while the fenders, hood, and grille retained the original N-series gray (although to this day the shade is debatable). Rear wheel lugs were increased to eight; the 9N and 2N had six. Front and rear wheel sizes remained the same.

The 8N (as well as earlier N-Series tractors) could also be converted to run six- and eight-cylinder Ford truck engines. This particular option was made possible by Funk Aviation of Coffeyville, Kansas. Beginning back in 1943, Funk had conversion kits for the Ford flathead six and from 1949 to 1950 for the V-8. (The Ford V-8 was rated at 100 horsepower.)The last conversion was for the valve-in-head straight six sometime after 1952. Depending on the powerplant desired, the kit included a channel iron frame from the bell housing to the axle carrier, strap extension for the radius arm (to move the front end forward), a larger thick core radiator, a hood spacer, and an extension for the steering. Funk specifications for the six-cylinder engines are listed below.

Funk's Standard Conversion Kit

Engine: Ford Industrial six-cylinder; bore 3.3 inches, stroke 4.4 inches; 226 ci piston displacement; compression ratio 6.7 to 1; speed rated continuos, 1,200 to 2,400 rpm

ARE A FUNDAMENTAL TRACTOR DESIGN

What's more, Dearborn Implements can be attached right up close to the tractor. This close coupling gives you a remarkably short outfit—a trend in farm equipment design that has been evident since the days of traction engines and gang plows. This is an important factor in the exceptional handling ease the Ford Tractor provides you.

The Ford Tractor Hydraulic Touch Control lever raises or lowers all lift type implements the same way. No need to manipulate levers on the implement—with the Ford Tractor you have complete control of working depth at your fingertips!

The next two pages explain why this arrangement of hydraulics and attachment permits the Ford Tractor to make so much more of its power.

Implements
lift and lower
at a touch

Most Dearborn Implements can be attached to the Ford Tractor in 60 seconds or less. The two lower lift arms are hydraulically controlled. Time saved in attaching or detaching can amount to several days a year.

The photo above demonstrates the use of the three-point hitch with hydraulics. The lower arms did the raising and lowering, while the upper link "pushed."

Tractor

Crankcase ....Heavy-duty cast
Radiator ....30 quarts
Speeds..1,200-2,400 rpm
Belt pulley ....1,358 rpm
PTO..545 rpm
Height..59.5 inches
Length ....78 inches
Weight.......................................2,760
Capacities
Cooling system ....21 quarts
Optional fuel tank ....8.5 gallons
Crankcase ....8 quarts

Funk's Model and Conversion Kit Specifications

(Specifications below are for the 8N, although special parts for the 9N could also be ordered)

Engine: Ford six-cylinder overhead valve; bore 3.56 inches, stroke 3.6 inches; 215 ci piston displacement; 180 foot-pounds of torque; compression ratio 7.0 to 1; 83 brake horsepower (engine) at 2,400 rpm. Fluid capacities: oil, 8 quarts, radiator, 17 quarts. Fuel capacity: main tank,10 gallons; optional tank,18 gallons. (Both Ford truck and automobile engines could also be used with modifications.)

Tractor

Wheelbase .... 79 inches
Length .... 124 inches
Height .... 55 inches
Width .... 65 inches
Rear tires (standard) 10x28
Rear tires (maximum) 11x28
Average front weight .... 1,100 pounds
Average rear axle weight (fluid)   2,100 pounds
Total average weight (with fluid)   3,200 pounds

Another company that offered conversion kits for the Ford tractor was the Glover Equipment Company of Milford, Illinois. Glover offered the Ford six-cylinder Industrial engine for the Ford-Ferguson (1940-47) and later for the Ford N-Series tractors from 1948 on. The kits were very similar to the Funk packages, enabling the Ford tractor to go from a two-bottom to a three-bottom plow capacity tractor.

8N Serial Numbers

(Serial and motor numbers are on the left-hand side of the engine block)
1947 .... 1 to 37907
1948 .... 37908 to 141369

SELECT THE METHOD YOU WANT
THIS **POWER** DELIVERED

① CONSTANT DRAFT CONTROL *and* **② IMPLEMENT POSITION CONTROL**

When disoing, subsoiling, plowing or doing similar jobs—you know the depth you want to work. Start off, and lower the Ford Tractor's Hydraulic Touch Control lever to get that depth. Once set, the hydraulic mechanism will automatically keep the implement at a depth to give a constant draft.

In other words, implements will work at the same depth in uniform soil even if your field is ridged or uneven! But if you encounter variations in soil, the implement can be maintained at the desired depth by moving the Hydraulic Touch Control lever up or down.

But say your field is smooth, yet soil conditions "vary all over the lot." Then flip the Selection Lever as shown in this picture to the "up" position. Now you are in Implement Position Control. No matter how much the soil varies this control is designed to maintain a constant working depth in a smooth field, automatically, without moving the Ford Tractor's Hydraulic Touch Control lev.

How many tractors have a hydraulic mechanism that gives you this choice at the flick of a lever? How many are designed to fit all of your soil and field surface conditions so well? Answer: Just one . . . Ford!

Fords sales literature highlighted the hydraulic system of the 8N, and paid particular attention to Constant Draft Control and Implement Position Control (the same basic features discussed with the 9N/2N). The photo above diagrams the hydraulic function with the two-bottom plow. The center of the photo shows the lever that actuated the hydraulic controls that was placed near the right-hand side of the operators seat for easy access. *Ford Brochure, 1951*

1949..141370 to 245636
1950..245637 to 343592
1951..343593 to 442034
1952..442035 to 524076

Specifications*
Engine: four-cylinder L head; 3.118-inch bore, 3.75-inch stroke; compression ratio 6 to 1; displacement 120 ci; 92 foot-pounds of torque at 1,500 rpm. Crankshaft is cast-steel, statically and dynamically balanced.

Bearing size
> Outer end bearings 2.25x1.6 inches
> Middle bearings 2.25x1.66 inches

Connecting rods: forgings crank pin pressure lubricated
Bearing size 2.1x1.125 inches

Pistons: Autothermic, aluminum alloy, cam ground,
off-set pin for added life

Piston rings: 3/32-inch top compression,
chrome-plated; 3/32-inch second compression
ring with light expander for quick break-in;
3/16-inch oil ring

Piston pin: full floating, 2.85x75 inches

Valves and guides: one-piece valve guides with
removable exhaust inserts
Transmission: Constant mesh, four speeds forward,
one reverse

Engine rpm

	1,500 rpm	1,750 rpm	2,000 rpm
1st gear	2.77 mph	3.23 mph	3.69 mph
2nd gear	3.56 mph	4.16 mph	4.75 mph
3rd gear	4.09 mph	5.72 mph	6.54 mph
4th gear	10.23 mph	11.93 mph	13.64 mph
Reverse	4.55 mph	5.31 mph	6.07 mph

Clutch: single-plate semi-centrifugal foot operated,
9 inches in diameter

Steering: automotive type with ball-nut gear

Cooling system: tube and fin pressure cap,
impeller water pump with prelubricated
bearing, fan diameter at 15.75 inches,
pump capacity at 15.4 gallons 1,500 rpm
per minute, coolant capacity at 12 quarts

Carburetor: single updraft plain-tube type, dust-proof construction equipped with accelerating well and economizer; Schebler, 7/8-inch adjustable; 10-gallon fuel capacity with 1 gallon in reserve

Air cleaner: oil bath with removable element for cleaning

Governor: centrifugal-type variable speed

Electrical system: two-brush generator, 20 amps and 142 watts at 1,500 rpm engine speed; regulator (voltage and current control); ignition-automatic spark advance with side-mounted distributor; safety starter; 80 ampere, 13-plate, 6-volt battery

Front wheels: standard-adjustable tread from 48 inches to 76 inches, 4.00x19 tires
Rear wheels: tread adjustable from 48 inches to 76 inchesin 4-inch steps; 10x28 tires standard

Brakes: internal expanding, operated by right foot

Hydraulic pump: Scotch yoke with four pistons, internally mounted; maximum pressure 1,500 pounds per square inch; delivery of up to 2.85 gallons per minute at 2,000 rpm

Overall measurements
Maximum height ....54.5 inches
Maximum length ....114.5 inches
Maximum width at 48 inches ..64.75 inches
Maximum width at 76 inches ..86 inches

Color: gray with red castings.
Specifications from 8N sales literature and operators manual, 1951.

Options and Extra Equipment
Lighting kit: original headlight kit includes two

sealed headlamps and all necessary wiring.
Taillight and license plate light also available.

Bumper: welded, rolled steel bumper was bolted to
the front axle to protect radiator grille.
Bumper was also outfitted with a hitch for
chain use. Adequate for pushing.

Tractor jack: lifted entire tractor off the ground
when used with Ford Tractor Hydraulic
Control lever. Maximum ground
clearance when fully raised was 3
feet. Constructed of welded tubing.

Front wheel conversion assembly: The larger front
disc and rim allowed the use of 6.00x16 tires
for heavy front end work such as with a
front-end loader for extended time periods.

Stabilizer assembly: Stabilizer arms were available
for situations such as middlebusting to ensure
a more rigid draft against side motion.

ASAE PTO conversion assembly: Converted the
Ford tractors PTO to meet ASAE standards.
The assembly included PTO extension,
safety shield, drawbar extension, and
drawbar stay braces for locking the hitch point.

Tire pump and gauge: Used engine compression to
fill implement, tractor, or automobile tires
out in the field. Sixteen-foot flexible hose
with brass fittings and air gauge.

Power take-off pulley assembly: The pulley
was designed to work in a right, left, or
down position. The 9-inch pulley with a
6 1/2-inch face put out 1,358 rpm at 2,000
engine rpm. Belt speed was 3,200 feet

The 8N and Dearborn economy plow. Ford *Brochure, 1951*

per minute. Equipped with tapered
roller bearings.

Half cabs: Available from Ford Motor Company's
tractor and implement division for 9N
through 900 Series tractors. Features of the
cabs included folding tops, rear drop
curtains, doors, engine compartment flaps,
and tilting windshield. It was made of
weather-proof canvas on a metal frame.

Aftermarket Accessories

•Both the ARPS Corporation of New Holstein, Wisconsin, and the Bombardier Company of Canada offered
track conversions for the N-Series tractors. The tracks
were used primarily for operation in snow, marshy land,
and soft ground. Oddly enough, the Bombardier system
was derived from the company's own snowmobile

design. The tracks gave the tractor added traction and maneuverability similar to four-wheel drive. Tracks were positioned around the rear wheels; an idler arm running from the tractor's differential supported the idler wheel that picked up the front portion of the track. Though I have been informed that Bombardier tracks were made primarily for the Ferguson tractors and ARPS for the Ford Ns, either company's tracks could be used for each tractor type. ARPS offered three track types: regular duty, heavy-duty, and extra heavy-duty. Various attachments were also available.

•The Tokheim Oil Tank and Pump Company of Fort Wayne, Indiana, produced an all-weather cab for the Ford-Ferguson and Ford N-Series tractors. The all-steel cab was easily installed by one person. The cab itself was an insulated one-piece cab, with all-steel turret top and corner posts and outfitted with adjustable windshield, door, and rear curtain.

•KR Wilson Company of Buffalo, New York, supplied a tractor dolly with built-in jacks for the Ford tractor. Wilson was well known to the Ford Motor Company as it already supplied factory-approved tools and equipment for Ford, Mercury, and Lincoln passenger cars. The dolly was designed to roll underneath and raise the tractor without the use of a conventional jack. Drivetrain units could be moved along the dolly independently with the use of a screw-operated slide that ran on the dolly's frame. Hold-down straps were also supplied to keep units tightly in place while being serviced.

•Not so much an everyday aftermarket accessory for the average farmer was the Gledhill Road Machinery Company's use of the Ford tractor to power its Convertible Road Roller. Gledhill Company literature stated that, "in a few minutes time it can be converted into a rubber tired tractor or back again to a road roller," giving its owner the benefit of two machines for the price of one. The roller was steered by the standard steering mechanism of the Ford tractor. The Road Roller came with a 3-ton roller with 600-pound water capacity in front rolls and a combination ballast tank and roof with 3,500-pound capacity totaling 5 tons! Rear rolls were also available, being installed in place of the rubber tires. Apparently the little Ford tractor had no trouble moving all that weight around. The Gledhill firm of Galion, Ohio, also made motor graders and shapers powered by Ford tractors.

Dearborn Implements
Dearborn Plows
Economy plows: two-bottom 12-inch, 14-inch, and 16-inch-"razor blade" shares
Standard plows: two-bottom 10-inch with Scotch bottoms; 12-inch with sod and clay bottoms; 14-inch general purpose or stubble bottoms
Two-way plows:16-inch right- and left-hand bottoms
Disc plow: 26-inch high carbon discs and adjustable scrapers

Dearborn Middlebuster
Row widths from 36 to 54 inches, and 12-inch blackland with 14-inch shares and 14-inch general-purpose bottoms

Dearborn Subsoiler
18-inch maximum penetration

Dearborn Field Cultivators
Nine spring tip shanks with 7-inch working width; reversible shovels, cultivator, and duck foot; sweeps were also available.

Dearborn Disc Harrows
Lift type: single-action disc harrows
Pull type: tandem disc harrows

Dearborn Bush and Bog Harrows
Lift type was offered with eight 20-inch or 22-inch notched discs with adjustable gang angles

Dearborn Spring Tooth Harrows

Spring tooth harrows were offered in two sections, 17 teeth with 6-foot cut or a three-section 25-tooth 9-foot cut. Both models could be operated easily by Ford tractors' Hydraulic Touch Control.

Dearborn Planters

Corn planter
Corn drill planter
Lister planters
Covington planters
Kelly planter attachments (used with Dearborn middle-buster or row crop frames)

Dearborn-Peoria Grain Drill

Fertilizer grain drill:13 single disc openers with 7-inch spacings

DEARBORN SIDE DELIVERY RAKE

This heavy duty rake does a clean job yet is remarkably "easy on the hay." That's because the reel is ground driven and has a motion that "pushes" the hay into the windrow rather than "whipping" it. The reel is raised and lowered by Ford Tractor Hydraulic Touch Control—a handy feature and a hay saving feature in many crop and ground conditions. Inverting action exposes stems, puts leaves inside windrow. Two leveling cranks permit easy reel adjustment. Raking width 8 feet.

DEARBORN SWEEP RAKE

With the Ford Tractor and this Dearborn Sweep Rake you can gather, lift, carry and unload 500 pounds of hay per trip. There's no hard work to it. Ford Tractor Hydraulic Touch Control does the lifting, no long heavy lever for you to work. Push-off rack automatically pushes off the load when teeth are lowered and tractor is backed. Good for handling shocked grain and corn, brush cuttings and orchard prunings.

DEARBORN WAGON

This wagon is a real bargain. Mass production enables it be sold at a surprisingly low price. Yet look what you get. Automotive type steering, tapered roller bearing equipped wheels, adjustable tie rods, heavy duty steering spindles—these features assure straight trailing, easy rolling. Swiveled reach, rocking bolster, double stop bars and welded steel chassis—these features assure long life. Sold without tires, box or rack. 15" wheels may be equipped with 5:50 x 15 or 6:00 x 16 or 6:50 x 16 tires. 15" wheels take 5:90 x 15 or 6:40 x 15 or 6:70 x 15 or 7:60 x 15 tires.

The 8N demonstrating its versatility with the side-delivery rake, sweep rake, and wagon, all Dearborn-made. The center photo shows the Model 8N doing some front-end work. The lift capacity, with the use of the Ford tractor Touch Control, was up to 500 pounds. *Ford Brochure, 1951*

Another 8N preparing a seed bed with the Dearborn made tandem disc harrow (lift-type). *Ford Brochure, 1951*

Dearborn Row Crop Cultivators

Rigid shank cultivator

Spring shank cultivator

List crop cultivator

Dearborn Weeder

Four row weeder spans 14 feet, 4 inches with 80 spring teeth

Dearborn Rotary Hoe

Lift type: 32 wheels, 10 teeth per wheel, 88-inch working width

Dearborn Mowers

Rear attached and side-mounted

Dearborn Rakes

Heavy-duty side delivery and sweep model

Dearborn-Wood Brothers Combines

Ford engine-powered or PTO drive; 6-foot cut was offered with bagger or bulk tank. Various options included cylinder speed control, windrow pickup, flax rolls, dual wheels, and reel attachment.

Dearborn-Wood Brothers Corn Harvester

One-row pull type, PTO drive; came with blower, rubber tires, and snapping bar

Dearborn-Wood Brothers Corn Picker

One-row pull type, 13 1/2x36-inch husking bed, spiral feed husking bed, and snapping roll

DEARBORN IMPLEMENTS PUT YOUR 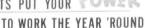 TO WORK THE YEAR 'ROUND

DEARBORN UTILITY BLADE

DEARBORN SCOOP

DEARBORN FIELD CULTIVATOR

DEARBORN SUBSOILER

DEARBORN ANGLE DOZER

DANUSER POST HOLE DIGGER

As you can see, the 8N could be used for just about anything on the one-tractor farm and then some. Because economy was, and still is, such an important part of the farm, the Ford tractor people decided to offer something new to the 8N to keep track of all that time and energy, the Proof-Meter. The Proof-Meter had five basic functions for keeping track of: engine speed, tractor travel speed in any gear, standard PTO shaft speed, belt pulley speed, and hours worked. Many who operated the 8N with the Proof-Meter agreed that if nothing else, they always knew when the tractor was due for normal lubrication and maintenance. *Ford Brochure, 1951*

Dearborn Crane

Danuser Post Hole Digger

Dearborn Lime and Fertilizer Spreader

Dearborn Cordwood Saw

Dearborn Wagon

Dearborn Scoop

Dearborn Loaders

Dearborn Blades

Dearborn Universal Frame and Attachments
Universal frame: used with Dearborn angle dozer, blade
snowplow, and "V" snowplow
Angle dozer blade: 60-degree angles both left and right
Blade snowplow and "V" snowplow same as angle dozer blade

CULTIVATING WITH FORD TRACTOR POWER

DEARBORN RIGID SHANK CULTIVATOR

With a Dearborn rear attached Cultivator you can really look ahead—way ahead—just as you do when you're plowing, discing or planting.

This means you can "stay ahead of the game" because you know in advance when you are going to hit a bend in the rows, a sticky spot, a hard spot, an obstruction, or where a couple of plants are out of line. As a result, you uproot fewer plants, you do a better job, and you can cultivate at higher speeds safely. But, that's not all . . .

You are not forced to sit in a cramped position with your eyes glued to the shovels as you "thread" thousands of plants-one-by-one between them. "Looking ahead" makes a big difference in the way you feel at the end of the day.

Ford Tractor Hydraulic Touch Control replaces hauling and heaving on long, heavy levers. *Dearborn Cultivators can be attached or detached in 60 seconds!* No nuts, no bolts, no wrenches needed. Wide variety of sweeps, shovels and points are available.

ROTARY HOE ATTACHMENT

Gets weeds in the row in early stages of crop growth. Two outer spiders act as a "screen," breaking up clods and allowing fine dirt thrown by shovels to sift into the row and cover small weeds. Higher speed cultivating is practical when rotary hoes are used. Front and rear depth adjustments. Sold separately.

Standard rotary hoe attachment (bottom); 8N pulling rigid-shank cultivator (top). *Ford Brochure, 1951*

CHAPTER 4

THE MODEL NAA
GOLDEN JUBILEE

With the upcoming fiftieth anniversary of the Ford Motor Company and the need to redesign components on the Ford tractor, it was only fitting that a totally new tractor should be unveiled. This new model arrived in 1953 and carried the name Golden Jubilee. (The 1954 model tractor was designated as NAA.)

Golden Jubilee-NAA Profile

New to the Jubilee-NAA model tractor was its more powerful Red Tiger engine. The new engine was the four-cylinder inline overhead valve, with a bore of 3.437 inches and stroke of 3.600 inches, displacement of 134 ci, 110 foot-pounds of torque at 1,400 rpm, and com-

At right is the 1953 Model Golden Jubilee. Because of the Ferguson lawsuit, Ford had to pay out close to 10 million dollars in patent infringements due to the continued use of the Ferguson System on the 8N tractor. The Golden Jubilee was named for the fiftieth Anniversary of the Ford Motor Company. The Jubilee was manufactured for two years (known as the Model NAA in 1954) and featured the Ford built hydraulic system and overhead valve Red Tiger four-cylinder engine. The most noticeable change on the Golden Jubilee was its styling. The grille retained its vertical bars, but the thicker center bar was done away with. The emblem logo was also changed, to a round protruding, "headlight" style and read "Golden Jubilee Model 1903-1953." The center of the emblem had the Ford oval with red background (earlier N's were blue) and a corn stalk in the center. This type of styling was very similar to Ford's cars and trucks. The scripted name Ford was retained along the hood and fenders. *Golden Jubilee sales literature, 1953*

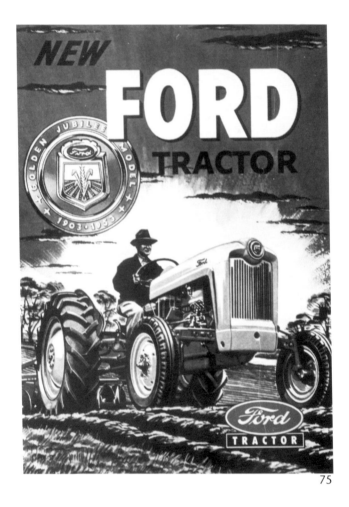

MORE CONTROLS than any other Tractor!

NO WONDE

HYDRAULIC HY-TROL

NEW TEMPERATURE GAUGE

OIL PRESSURE GAUGE

NEW EXACTO-SPEED THROTTLE

PROOF-METER

AMMETER

SAFETY STARTER

OUTLET FOR:
HYDRAULIC REMOTE
CYLINDER CONTROL*
BOOSTER CYLINDERS*
HYDRAULIC SELEC-TROL*

POSITIVE, EASY TO OPERATE CLUTCH

DUO-SERVO BRAKES

HYDRAULIC TOUCH CONTROL LEVER

PTO LEVER

HYDRAULIC SELECTOR LEVER

DUAL BRAKE LOCK

*Sold Separately

LOOK AT WHAT YOU HAVE TO WORK WITH...

The difference between an easy-handling, smooth-working tractor that really does a job and a man-killing brute is largely a matter of how well and how easily you can control its operation. The more things you can get done just by touching a knob or lever, the easier the job is on *you*. The more jobs controlled automatically, the better the work you'll do.

Also, the closer watch you can keep on the way your tractor is running, the easier it is to keep it in tiptop condition, and the less danger there is of breakdowns. That's why the *number* of controls and gauges on a Ford Tractor, their *convenient location* and *ease of use* are so important. In sizing up the new Ford Tractor take a look at all you have to work *with*.

A view from the top of the Jubilee's operators platform. The PTO lever was mounted on the left-hand side of the drivers seat; the hydraulic control lever on the right. In addition to the Touch Control, Constant Draft and Implement Position Controls, the Jubilee would also feature a "Live-Action" hydraulic system. "Live" because the hydraulic lines were filled with oil at all times for almost instantaneous response. The remote cylinder also became available on the Jubilee models, allowing the operation of a myriad of tools on the farm. *Sales brochure photo, 1953*

pression ratio of 6.6 to 1. Ford touted the large bore, short-stroke engine as being more efficient and longer lasting, mainly because the design increased power with less piston travel, creating less friction and wear on internal parts. The new Red Tiger also featured freely rotating exhaust valves to reduce valve sticking, cast-alloy sleeves for longer cylinder life, and a newly designed crankshaft. A PTO was standard while the "live" (independent) PTO was optional.

The ignition system was basically the same as that of the 8N with its side-mounted distributor, automatic spark advance, and so on. The electrical system on the Jubilee-NAA utilized the two-brush generator driven by V-belt (rated 20 amps at 1,650 rpm), a generator regulator, and six-volt battery. The carburetor, referred to as the "New Fuel-Saver," was the single updraft type with idle speed/fuel adjustment and main fuel jet adjustment. Other features such as brakes and steering remained identical to the 8N.

One of the biggest changes from the 8N to the Golden Jubilee-NAA was the hydraulic system. Because of the Ferguson lawsuit, Ford was forced to design its own hydraulic system. The so-called "solid system" was developed specifically for the Golden Jubilee-NAA ("solid" because it held oil in the lines at all times) and featured a variety of new functions. Oil in the lines at all times gave the operator split-second response with no waiting for lines to fill. Ford coined the term "Live-Action" with regard to their new hydraulic system and compared the older version to that of hand priming a pump, as opposed to simply turning on a spigot with the new.

Another feature of the new system was Hy-Trol (hydraulic control valve), a feature that enabled the operator to vary the flow of oil in the lines to suit his or her specific needs. Turning the knob clockwise on the Hy-Trol valve increased the flow of oil to the lift cylinder; counter clockwise had the opposite effect. The control valve was located at the rear of the pump next to the coil. The new system also made it easier to use around the farm for a variety of tasks. With the use of the remote cylinder, power tools and other types of machinery could be operated. The remote cylinder was connected via quick-coupling hose lines to the remote cylinder control valve and could be operated either manually or automatically. Booster cylinders were also available for rear-mounted loaders, almost doubling the loaders' lift capacity.

With the Touch Control lever, both front- and rear-mounted tools could be operated without the use of a second hydraulic pump. The handy Selec-Trol valve instantly diverted the flow of oil to either the front or rear of the tractor, enabling the lever to operate machinery at both ends (not simultaneously).

Probably the most obvious change to the Ford tractor was its physical appearance. The Golden Jubilee-NAA took on a totally different look, reflecting the styling that was so prevalent in the 1950s. While the new model Ford retained the scripted logo on the hood and rear fenders, the emblem on the top of the radiator went from the standard oval logo to the fiftieth anniversary emblem. The emblem was round, red, and read, "Golden Jubilee Model 1903-1953." The hood itself took on a streamlined look for improved crop visibility, with the radiator cap now hidden under the hood, up front behind the emblem housing.

Serial Numbers for the Jubilee and NAA

(Serial number is located on left side of transmission case at starter motor; earliest production models had serial numbers on front left corner of engine block, just below the manifold on a flat casting spot)

Beginning numbers
1953..1
1954..77475

Specifications for the Jubilee and NAA*

Engine: four-cylinder overhead valve; bore 3.437 inches, stroke 3.600 inches; displacement 134 ci; compression 6.6 to 1

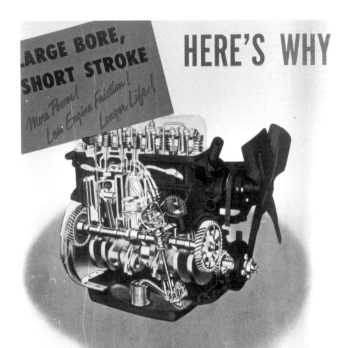

LARGE BORE, SHORT STROKE

More Power! Less Engine Friction! Longer Life!

HERE'S WHY

When you check into the inside features of Ford's new "Red Tiger" engine, you will see why it delivers so much more in the way of power, economy and long life—why it sets a *new high* in all-around tractor engine performance.

The secret is the large bore, short stroke design that develops extra power with less piston travel, less friction and wear—transforms more fuel power into work power! But,

this is just one advantage, although an extremely important one. There's much more.

All the way through, you will find outstanding features in this new engine. Some are shown on the next page. There are many more that can't be pictured here, but contribute greatly to easier servicing, plus the kind of on-the-job dependability you want and need in a tractor engine.

12

The Jubilee and NAA models used the Red Tiger engine, the very same engine that would be found on the "new breed" of Ford tractors, the 600 and 700 Series models, that were brought out in 1955. *Sales brochure photo, 1953*

Crankshaft: precision alloy, statically and dynamically balanced

Main bearing

Front...2.5x1.5 inches
Middle ....2.5x1.75 inches
Rear... 2.5x1.64 inches

Connecting rods: forged steel, bearing size 2.3x1.03 inches

Pistons: Autothermic aluminum alloy, cam ground

Rings: chrome-plated

Piston pin: full-floating, lubricated from bearings

Valves and guides: overhead valves and removable cast-chrome-moly steel alloy exhaust inserts, removable valve guides, and chrome-moly closed coil springs

Carburetor: single updraft plain tube type equipped with accelerating well and economizer (Schebler, 7/8-inch adjustable)

Fuel capacity: 11 gallons with 1 3/4 gallon in reserve tank

Air cleaner: oil bath with removable lower element for cleaning

Cooling system: tube and fin radiator with pressure cap; impeller pump with prelubricated bearings; fan diameter, 15 3/4 inches; pump capacity 16 gallons per minute at 1,400 rpm

Governor: centrifugal, variable speed; fully enclosed and mounted on the crankshaft

Electrical system: two-brush generator, 1,650 rpm, 20 amps, capacity 160 watts; regulator-voltage and current control; ignition, side-mounted distributor with automatic spark advance; safety starter was standard; battery, 80 ampere/hour, 13 plates, 6-volt

Transmission: constant mesh, four-speed

Clutch: single plate, semi-centrifugal foot-operated, 9-inch plate

Steering: ball-nut gear, automotive type

Front wheels: adjustment of tread from 48 to 76 inches with 4.00x19 tires (standard) and 5.50x16 tires (optional)

Rear wheels: adjustment of tread from 48 to 76 inches in 4-inch steps. 10x28 tires (standard) and 11x28 tires (optional)

Brakes: internal expanding, individually or simultaneously

Hydraulic pump: vane type, constant running mounted on engine. Maximum operating pressure 2,000 pounds per square inch; capacity adjustable from 2.25 to 5 gallons per minute by Hy-Trol valve on pump

Weight: approximately 2,510 pounds

Measurements

Wheelbase at 48-inch tread ......73 7/8 inches
Maximum height ....57 1/4 inches
Maximum length ....120 3/4 inches
Maximum width at 48-inch tread 64 3/4 inches
Maximum width at 76-inch tread 86 inches
Specifications and data taken from Ford tractor manuals and literature, 1954

A factory cutaway of the Jubilee. *Ford Brochure, 1953*

Options

Lighting kit: Kits included two sealed-beam headlights along with switch and wiring. Implement light was also available with frosted beam. Taillight and license plate light were available at extra cost.

Bumper: Made of steel, both welded and riveted, attached to front axle, complete with hitch. Bumper also protected radiator grille.

Live PTO: All tractor engine power goes to PTO with no interruption.

Power take-off pulley assembly: Easily attached to rear of differential and operates right, left, or in down position; 9-inch pulley with 6 1/2-inch face develops 1,358 rpm at 2,000 rpm engine speed. Belt speed is 3,200 feet per minute.

ASAE PTO conversion assembly: Converted the Ford tractor PTO to meet ASAE standards. Assembly included PTO extension, safety shield, drawbar extension, and stay braces that properly positioned and locked the hitch point.

Selec-Trol Valve: For the operation of standard front-end loaders and rear-mounted tools from the built-in hydraulic system.

Remote hydraulic unit: Included control valve and operating lever, Dearborn ASAE double-acting cylinder, and break-away coupling with hoses. Could be used for operating a variety of tools around the farm and adjusting levers and cranks on implements.

Stabilizer assembly: Stabilizer arms for straight line action such as in middlebusting or planting.

Front wheel conversion assembly: Larger front-wheel disc and rim for the use of 6.00x16 tires for heavy front-end work (i.e., using a front-end loader).

Tire pump and gauge set: Pump that operated from engine compression for a variety of uses on the farm where air was needed. Came with 16-foot flexible hose, brass connector, and air pressure gauge.

Half cabs: Available from Ford's tractor and implement division for 9N through 900 Series tractors. Features of the cabs included folding tops, rear drop curtains, doors, engine compartment flaps, and tilting windshield. Made of weatherproof canvas on a metal frame.

Dearborn Implements for Jubilee-NAA
Dearborn Plows

Economy plows: two-bottom 12-inch, 14-inch, and 16-inch-"razor blade" shares
Standard plows: two-bottom 10-inch with Scotch bottoms; 12-inch with sod and clay bottoms; 14-inch general purpose or stubble bottoms Two-way plows:16-inch right- and left-hand bottoms Disc plow: 26-inch high car bon discs and adjustable scrapers

Dearborn Middlebuster

Row widths from 36 to 54 inches, and 12-inch blackland with 14-inch shares and 14-inch general purpose bottoms

Dearborn Subsoiler

18-inch maximum penetration

Half Cab Accessories FOR GREATER COMFORT!

FOLDING TOP—The folding top gives added protection against the cold . . . doubles as a summer sun shade, too. It attaches quickly and easily, folds out of the way just as fast. Three types available . . . one to fit each Half Cab model. Sold separately.

Kit No. 231057—for Ford 600, 800, NAA, 2N, 8N and 9N
Kit No. 231048—for Ford 700 and 900 Tractors
Kit No. 231055—for Fordson Major Diesel Tractors

REAR DROP CURTAIN—Rear drop curtains give complete all-around protection. With the addition of top and drop curtain units to the Half Cab the operator is completely enclosed . . . more completely protected against the weather. Sold separately.

Kit No. 231056—for Ford 600, 700, 800, 900, NAA, 2N, 8N and 9N
Kit No. 231050—for Fordson Major Diesel Tractors

NOW! KITS FOR USE WITH TRACTORS EQUIPPED WITH INDUSTRIAL LOADERS AND REAR MOUNTED POWER DIGGERS

KIT NO. 231257—With this kit, Industrial operators can now have Half Cab protection when operating Ford 600 or 800 Series Tractors equipped with Industrial Loaders.

KIT NO. 231258—A companion kit which converts Half Cab Kit No. 231257, at left, for use on Ford 600 and 800 Series Tractors when equipped with a rear mounted power digger.

SEE YOUR FORD TRACTOR DEALER!

One of the many extras offered for the Ford N-Series tractors was this half-cab to protect against the elements. The photo clearly shows the utility and various versions that could be purchased. This particular style of cab was produced by Ford and even included canvas engine compartment flaps for generating heat to the driver in the wintertime. *Ford flyer, 1958*

4-WHEEL STABILITY . . . *Row Crop Ability*

You get stability, ease and accuracy of steering that only wide-spaced front wheels can give. Front and rear wheels can be spaced in 4-inch steps from 48 to 76 inches to fit just about any row crop. Wheels on one side can be set wide with wheels on the opposite side set narrow—valuable for haymaking and hillside work.

EASY-READ PROOF-METER . . . *Replaces Guesswork with Facts!* Even the most experienced tractor operator normally operates by hit-or-miss methods because he has no sure check of engine operation. The PROOF-METER supplies this missing link. It registers engine speed, tractor travel speed, PTO speed, belt pulley speed and hours of tractor operation. Just a glance now and then tells you the facts that help you do better work, prolong equipment life, make more money.

BUILT-IN HYDRAULIC SYSTEM . . . *Standard*

Performs as *part* of the Ford Tractor, and all other operations of the tractor are coordinated with it. This built-in system gives you both Constant Draft Control and Implement Position Control. Since the hydraulic system is standard, Dearborn Implements are engineered to take advantage of it.

POWER TAKE-OFF . . . *Regular Equipment*

Operates PTO-driven mowers, post hole diggers, sprayers, dusters. Can be quickly converted to drive any PTO-operated machine that has standard ASAE drive coupling. New powerful "Red Tiger" engine improves performance of PTO-driven machines—Proof-Meter shows proper PTO speed.

More illustrated features of the Jubilee and NAA. In addition to extras like the half-cab, other optional equipment included lighting kits, bumpers, live PTO, stabilizer kits, a front wheel conversion assembly, and the Selec-Trol valve for operating both front-end loaders and rear mounted tools from the hydraulic system. Ford *Brochure, 1953*

Dearborn Field Cultivators
Nine spring tip shanks with 7-inch working width. Reversible shovels, cultivator, and duck foot sweeps were also available

Dearborn Disc Harrows
Lift type: single-action disc harrows
Pull type: tandem disc harrows

Dearborn Bush and Bog Harrows
Lift type was offered with eight 20-inch or 22-inch notched discs with adjustable gang angles

Dearborn Spring Tooth Harrows
Spring tooth harrows were offered in two sections, 17 teeth with 6-foot cut or a three section 25-tooth 9-foot cut. Both models could easily be operated by Ford tractors' Hydraulic Touch Control

Dearborn Planters
Corn planter
Corn drill planter
Lister planters
Covington planters
Kelly planter attachments (used with Dearborn middle-buster or row crop frames)

Dearborn-Peoria Grain Drill
Fertilizer grain drill:13 single-disc openers with 7-inch spacings

Dearborn Row Crop Cultivators
Rigid shank cultivator
Spring shank cultivator
List crop cultivator

Dearborn Weeder
Four-row weeder spans 14 feet, 4 inches with 80 spring teeth

The wheelbase of the Jubilee and NAA was lengthened and over-all weight of the tractor increased to enhance stability and create a low center of gravity for better "hugging" ability, unlike the earlier N models.
Brochure, 1953

BIGGER... HEAVIER... STURDIER ... *Throughout*

The entire tractor has been designed with the extra size, weight and strength to match the increased power of the new Ford Tractor "Red Tiger" engine. Wheelbase has been lengthened, adding greatly to all-around working stability. The greater weight is properly distributed over this longer wheelbase to increase traction and ground-hugging ability.

Throughout the tractor, parts have been strengthened, given added size and weight which means additional dependability and longer life. The differential and rear axle have been improved to effectively transfer the tractor's engine power into extra field performance. Gears are bigger, parts are sturdier. Here is a tractor built for a long lifetime of hard work!

Power-Saving Transmission
Precision-cut helical gears and tapered roller bearings reduce friction and power loss. Sturdier gears and parts and rigid transmission assembly resist deflections or common to less well-built transmissions. New slow reverse gear for more positive control, greater safety.

Heavy-Duty Front Axle
The two longer, stronger front axle permits extension of front wheels to full 76-inch spacing without reversing the wheels. This results in more positive, easier steering. Heavy-duty radius rods give strong axle support at all wheel spacings.

Broad Base for Overhanging Loads
You get more load-lifting stability and safety with the new Ford Tractor because the front and rear wheels are farther apart. This longer wheelbase permits use of increased capacity implements—helps to get more work done safely and easily.

Dearborn Rotary Hoe
Lift type: 32 wheels, 10 teeth per wheel, 88-inch working width

Dearborn Mowers
Rear-attached and side-mounted

Dearborn Rakes
Heavy-duty side delivery and sweep model

Dearborn-Wood Brothers Combines
Ford engine-powered or PTO drive, 6-foot cut, was offered with bagger or bulk tank. Various options included cylinder speed control, windrow pickup, flax rolls, dual wheels, and reel attachment

Dearborn-Wood Brothers Corn Harvester
One-row pull type, PTO drive, came with blower, rub-

ber tires, and snapping bar

Dearborn-Wood Brothers Corn Picker
One-row pull type, 13 1/2x36-inch husking bed, spiral feed husking bed, and snapping roll

Dearborn Crane

Danuser Post Hole Digger

Dearborn Lime and Fertilizer Spreader

Dearborn Cordwood Saw

Dearborn Wagon

Dearborn Scoop

Dearborn Loaders

Dearborn Blades

Dearborn Universal Frame and Attachments: Universal frame: used with Dearborn angle dozer, blade snowplow, and "V" snowplow Angle dozer blade: 60-degree angles both left and right Blade snowplow and "V" snowplow same as angle dozer blade

Dearborn Peanut Digger and Windrower:
Two-row lift type, digs and windrows; capacity, two acres per hour

Dearborn Hay Baler:
One-man baler, 26-horsepower engine plunger type. Rotary spring finger pickup auger and sweeparm feed into bale chamber; 36-inch or 42-inch sliced bales with twine tie. Up to eight bales per minute. Wagon tongue and extension chute were sold separately.

CHAPTER 5

THE HUNDRED SERIES

Beginning in 1955, Ford was no longer a "one tractor" company. With competition growing throughout the industry, Ford needed to expand its line, introducing not only four new models but also two different power classes. The 600-Series became the new all-purpose model, resembling an improved NAA, but with new features and equipment. The 700-Series, also introduced in 1955, was the tricycle version of the 600 and was equipped with the same powerplant. The 800-Series served as the beefed-up version of the 600 with three-plow power, while the 900-Series, also a tricycle model, was introduced as a row crop version of the 800. (The 700 was the first U.S.-built tricycle row crop tractor by Ford.)

The expansion of the line was welcome news to Ford tractor owners everywhere. In fact, many wondered why it had taken Ford so long to offer a row crop model, particularly because of International Harvester's success with the Farmall in the 1930s. Whatever the reasons were for the delay are unknown. Suffice it to say that Ford was better late than never.

In 1955, Ford introduced its first tricycle tractor for row crop farming. Above is the Model 740, a two-plow tractor suitable for four-row equipment. The 740 was the only model in the 700 Series. The power plant was the same offered in the 600 series, the 134 ci Red Tiger engine with four-speed transmission. You will note that the grille on both 600 and 700 Series tractors is almost identical to the NAA, and headlights were now standard. *Ford Brochure, 1955*

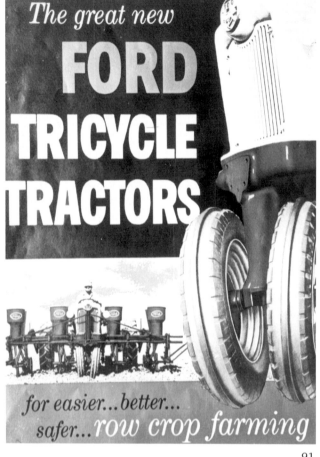

The great new

FORD
TRICYCLE
TRACTORS

for easier... better... safer... row crop farming

...uuuuues inese great tractors, t

THE 800 SE

Here's full 3-plow power in 4-wheel version. Two outstanding up the 800 Series and offer su 5-speed transmission, live powe cubic inch "Red Tiger" Pow'r-Pl as on all Ford Tractors, Ford's f hydraulic system. Just watch the one of these great tractors.

THE 600 SERIES

Low cost 2-plow power that gets far more done! That's Ford's 600 Series. Available in three models, the 600 Ford Tractors make ideal second tractors on larger acreages, real work producers and time savers as the first tractor on smaller farms. These tractors pay off best for you in handling a wide variety of farm jobs at low cost.

Top-left is the 800 Series All-Purpose model tractor, equipped with the 172 ci Red Tiger engine and five-speed transmission. Rated at 45 horsepower, the 800's became Ford's first three-plow tractors. Below right is the all-purpose 600 with the identical standard equipment as the 700, less the dual tricycle wheel and differences in crop height, wheelbase, and length. (the 600-800 series were roughly six inches lower than the 700-900). *Ford Brochure, 1955*

But by 1958, Ford tractor sales had fallen to less than 15 percent of the market, prompting engineers to redesign the 600-900 Series and introduce new models in that same year. Styling and an increase in horsepower was just the beginning with the 601, 701, 801, and 901 Series tractors that were produced from 1958 to 1962. New features such as power steering, diesel-powered engines, the optional two-range over-under transmission with four speeds, and the Select-O-Speed transmission for on-the-go shifting were other advances noted in the four-reworked-tractor series. One other interesting model brought out by Ford in 1959 was the 501 Series, a one-row off-set tractor that was actually a redesign of the 600. It has been reported that not many of the 501 Series tractors were sold due to its propensity for tipping over under certain conditions. The stiff competition from the rival Farmall A didn't help either. Needless to say, however, the 501 Series still has a great following today and is sought after by collectors.

600, 700, 800, and 900 Series Profile

The 600 Series tractor was actually quite similar to the Model NAA. Its powerplant was the same 132-cubic-inch, 31-horsepower Red Tiger engine, and outside of some new features, it was the same tractor. The new features included an improved four-speed transmission; a five-speed was available by special order. A new "live" PTO also became available in addition to the transmission-driven one, with optional double-action remote cylinders used with the live hydraulic system. Model numbers in the 600 Series denoted whether they operated with a particular transmission, PTO, or hydraulic system, yielding five different models.

The 700 Series consisted of one row crop model, based primarily on the 600. It was Ford's first U.S.-produced tricycle tractor. The 700 was only available with the transmission-driven PTO and a four-speed transmission; the powerplant was the same as the 600. In addition, all electrical, fuel, cooling, and hydraulic systems were the same as the 600. The only real difference was the front dual tricycle wheels and additional clearance height required for row crop work. Also, like the 600 Series, the 700 was a two-plow tractor used for not only two-row, but four-row operations as well. Just about all the aforementioned Dearborn implements could be used with the 700 row cropper.

Probably the most welcomed addition to the tractor line in 1955 was the 800 Series. Just as the 700 was the first tricycle tractor built in the United States, the 800 became the first U.S.-built three-plow tractor. The powerplant on the 800 was the big 45-horsepower, 172-cubic-inch Red Tiger gas engine. The 800 could be ordered with the four- or five-speed transmission, transmission-driven or live PTO, and the live hydraulic system with three-point linkage and double-acting remote cylinders. With these different options available, four models made up the 800 Series.

ABOVE AND BELOW
Three-quarter frontal view of the 700 and 900 Series row croppers. If you think your seeing double it's very understandable. The only differences between the two tractors: 0.4 inches of length; 0.7 inches of crop clearance; 84 pounds of weight; tire sizes are 5.50x16 (front) and 11x28 (rear) for the 700 and 6x16 (front) and 12x28 (rear) for the 900; four-speed transmission on the 700 and a five-speed with the 900; and the difference in engine size. Power adjusted wheels was standard on both 900 Series tractors; the live PTO was standard on the model 960 only. The one 700 Series model came with the standard four-speed and transmission PTO with power adjusted wheels optional. *Brochure photo, 1955*

Rounding out the line was the 900 Series tricycle row cropper, equipped with the same powerplant as the 800s. The five-speed transmission, live PTO, and power-adjusted wheels, however, were standard. Other standard features included sealed-beam headlights and a Rest-O-Ride seat (also offered on the 700), giving the operator "real arm-chair comfort." The seat action could be adjusted for weight and height convenience. There were actually two models offered in the 900 Series, the 950 and 960, the only real difference being that the 960 came with live PTO and a double 9-inch clutch. The 950 had the standard transmission-driven PTO and a single 10-inch clutch.

Stylistically speaking, all four series tractors looked quite similar, though the 600 and 800 models were a bit wider and lower to the ground for obvious reasons (the difference between row crop and utility operations). The color was still gray with red castings, a scheme that began with the 8N and would continue until the arrival of the "blue line" tractors in 1962. Emblems and logos were still mounted above the grille, with the series number on top, the Ford oval under the series number, and a stalk of corn in the middle. The center of the emblem is reminiscent of those that were carried on Ford-produced cars and trucks of that era.

Serial Numbers for 600, 700, 800, and 900 Series Tractors
1954...1
1955...10615
1956...77271
1957...116368

Specifications for 600 and 800 Series Tractors*
Engine: four-cylinder, inline overhead valve gasoline; bore and stroke (600 Series) 3.44x3.60 inches, (800) 3.90x3.60 inches, piston displacement (600) 134 ci, (800) 172 ci,

You'll appreciate the extra comfort and convenience features you get in a

FORD!

Easy to handle VARI-WEIGHTS

Ford weights come in *easy on*, easy off segments that are convenient to handle. One man can attach them without heavy lifting or straining, and without use of a hoist. When properly used, these weights can help you to take full advantage of the tractor's power without the neccesity of having to carry around a lot of extra built-in weight when not needed.

REAR WHEEL WEIGHTS

Rear wheel weights for Ford Workmaster tractors are made in 30-pound segments. Each wheel takes up to 12 of these easy-to-handle segments.

FRONT WHEEL WEIGHTS

Front wheel weights are also easy to handle. They're made in 50-pound segments, 2 to a wheel.

FRONT WEIGHT BOX

Holds up to six 48-pound segments for adding weight to front of tricycle type row crop tractors.

- **PROOF-METER**—Lets you tell at a glance engine speed, hours worked, travel speed, proper engine speed for PTO or belt pulley work.

- **POWER STEERING**—Standard on row crop models, optional on others.

- **POWER ADJUSTED REAR WHEELS**—Optional on all models.

- **SWINGING DRAWBAR**—Provides good maneuverability and easy turning with pull type implements.

- **POWERFUL BEAM HEADLIGHTS**—Concentrated narrow beam gives far-reaching visibility at night.

- **SAFETY STARTER**—Ignition key must be "on" and tractor in neutral ("park" on Select-O-Speed models) before engine can be started.

- **DEPENDABLE OVERSIZE BRAKES**—Provide quick-action braking for maneuverability and safety.

COMFORTABLE POSITION IN SEAT

Your position in the seat of a Ford tractor is comfortable and relaxing. The position and angle of the steering wheel are such that your hands and arms remain in a restful, natural position.

EASY TO GET ON AND OFF

Open design and wide, low step plates help to take the inconvenience out of getting on and off the tractor. There's no climbing over hitches, no scraped shins.

Vari-Weights were a popular option on all the 600-900 Series models. As shown in the photo, placement of the 12 30-pound segments could be used either all together or individually, depending on the weight needed. Front wheel weights were also available. *Ford Brochure, 1955* compression ratio (600) 6.60 to 1, (800) 6.75 to 1; maximum speed (no load) (600) 2,200 rpm; (800) 2,400 rpm

Air cleaner: oil bath with removable lower element for cleaning

Oil filter: Full-flow

Transmission: (Models 620, 630, and 640) constant mesh four-speed, helical gear; (Models 650, 660, 820, 850, and 860) constant mesh five-speed helical gear

Gear ratios for four-speed transmissions

1st gear: 11.00 to 1
2nd gear: 8.56 to 1
3rd gear: 6.22 to 1
4th gear: 2.98 to 1
Reverse: 10.04 to 1

Gear ratios for five-speed transmissions

1st gear: 17.55 to 1
2nd gear: 11.04 to 1
3rd gear: 8.31 to 1
4th gear: 6.02 to 1
5th gear: 3.38 to 1
Reverse: 10.29 to 1

Clutch: (Models 620, 630, and 640) single-plate 9-inch; (Model 650) single-plate 10-inch; (Model 660) double-plate 9-inch; (Models 820 and 850) single-plate 10-inch; (Model 860) double-plate 9-inch. Model 840 featured four-speed with over-under transmission; six forward speeds and two reverse.

Steering: anti-reversible, combination bevel gears and worm sector

FORD'S NEW
front mounted equipment
FOR OUTSTANDING ROW CROP PERFORMANCE

2 and 4-row cultivators

Ford's new 2 and 4-row cultivators head the list of all new front mounted implements for use with the 700 and 900 Ford Tractors. Available in either spring shank or spring trip models, these cultivators have an extra sturdy, easily attached frame and many outstanding features. All gangs have independent action to follow uneven ground, provide *real* precision cultivating. Extra attachments such as the rotary hoe, disc hiller or spread arch increase their versatility.

2 and 4-row planter attachments

Designed for mounting on the 2 or 4-row cultivator frame, Ford's new drill planter attachments are of the "unit type" construction with independently floating runner frames for uniform planting. Offered with either corn or corn and cotton hoppers, Ford's drill planters feature such advancements as extra big, one-bushel capacity hoppers; hopper and plate design that means less seed cracking; quick, easy seed plate changing without emptying hoppers, and many more.

Fertilizer and side dresser attachments (not shown) are designed for maximum usability. Planter fertilizer attachments can also be used as side dressers, while hoppers are interchangeable between both fertilizer and side dresser units.

1-row pickers are quickly and easily mounted on Ford's new tricycle tractors and on Ford's 4-wheel models, too. Advanced features include exceptional picking ability; gentle handling of ears to prevent corn loss; fast, positive hydraulic control of gathering points and automatic wagon elevator shut-off when gathering points are raised. Corn harvester model also available.

2-row pickers are mounted on the 700 or 900 Ford Tractors in short order. This big capacity picker harvests cleaner corn and more of it, has outstanding picking ability. It offers the same advanced design features as the 1-row model, including gentle handling of ears for less corn loss, instant hydraulic control, elevator shut-off and many more.

The 700 and 900 row croppers in the field. *Ford Brochure, 1955*

Cooling system: tube and fin radiator with pressure cap. Impeller water pump; prelubricated bearings; three-blade fan, 15.687-inch to 15.812-inch diameter. System capacity, 15 quarts

Fuel system: gravity flow single updraft carburetor; fuel tank capacities: (600) 11 gallons, (800) 14 gallons

Electrical system: two-brush shunt wound generator (20-amp,140-watt capacity); 6-volt battery; relay type regulator; automatic starter motor with safety switch; automatic centrifugal spark advance distributor

Hydraulic system: live action piston pump with gear drive; maximum pressure is 2,000 pounds psi; 4 gallons per minute at 2,000 engine rpm capacity; Implement Position or Constant Draft control

Brakes: internal expanding, mechanically controlled

Rear wheels: (600 Series) 11.28x28 standard; (800) 12.00x28 standard

Front wheels: (600) 5.50x16 standard; (800) 6.60x16 standard

Overall measurements
Wheelbase at 52-inch
    tread width ....74.5 inches
Overall length at 52-inch tread width
    (600 and 800) ....120.83 inches
Overall width at 52-inch
    tread width ....63.9 inches
Front tread width, All-purpose
    tractors ....52 to 76 inches
Rear tread width, All-purpose
    tractors ....52 to 76 inches

Front tread width, Special Utility
　　　tractors ....52 to 76 inches
Rear tread width, Special Utility
　　　tractors ....48 to 76 inches
Rear tread width, Power Adjust
　　　wheels ....56 to 84 inches
Turning circle diameter
　　　(with brakes) ....17 feet, 10 inches

Approximate shipping weight: depending on model and series
from 2,462 to 2,991 pounds
*Specifications and data obtained from operators
manuals and sales literature, 1957.*

Specifications for 700 and 900 Series (Tricycle) Tractors*

Engine: (700 Series) four-cylinder overhead valve
　　　gasoline; bore 3.44 inches, stroke 3.6 inches;
　　　134 ci displacement; compression ratio 6.6
　　　to 1. (900 Series) bore 3.90-inch, stroke 3.60;
　　　172 ci piston displacement; compression
　　　ratio 6.75 to 1. Maximum speed (no load),
　　　(700) 2,200 rpm; (900) 2,400 rpm

Air cleaner: oil bath with removable lower element
　　　for cleaning

Oil filter: full flow

Transmission: four-speed, constant mesh

Clutch: foot-operated, single-plate 9-inch

Steering: anti-reversible, combination bevel gears and worm sector

Cooling system: tube and fin radiator with pressure
　　　cap. Impeller water pump; prelubricated
　　　bearings; three-blade fan, 15.687 to
　　　15.812-inch diameter. System capacity, 15 quarts

ADVANCED HYDRAULIC CONTROL WITH FORD'S LIVE-ACTION

hydraulic system

It works with Ford's 3-point hitch for easier... better...quicker farming

Ford's built-in, live-action hydraulic system does *more* for you in many ways. It's easier, because you control mounted implements at the touch of a lever. It's faster, because it's a solid system, with lines and valves filled with oil at all times for quick, smooth, positive response. It means better work because you have accurate, split second control. Teamed with one of the many mounted implements designed for Ford's famous 3-point hitch, it provides better all-around job performance.

And there's more to Ford's hydraulic story. You have a choice of hydraulic speeds to suit the job with 5-position Hy-Trol. And a handy remote cylinder unit (sold separately) lets you control all types of pulled equipment hydraulically.

Fast...smooth ...accurate implement control at a touch of this lever

Choose the hydraulic action you need

CONSTANT DRAFT CONTROL

With Ford you can have the hydraulic action needed for any job at the flick of a lever. First, there's Constant Draft Control which permits the mounted implement to adjust to variations in the draft of the soil—instantly and automatically. This control translates engine power into better work performance, means top engine operating efficiency.

IMPLEMENT POSITION CONTROL

Where fields are smooth and fairly level, but soil conditions "vary all over the lot," then move the Selector Lever to Implement Position Control. In this position, the hydraulic system maintains a constant working depth for your implement—automatically. It means more uniform depth of plows and other implements for a better job.

Carried over from the NAA is the same hydraulic system. *Ford Brochure, 1955*

Above illustrates the power-adjusted wheels system introduced with the Model 960 row cropper in 1955. Like the literature said, "No more jacks, no more hoists, no more tugging and straining to change wheel tread." All one had to do was loosen up the wheel lugs, set the brake, and let the tractor "power spin" the wheels to the desired setting. In fact, settings could be made in half-inch increments between 56 and 76 inches. *Ford Brochure, 1955*

Fuel tank: 14 gallon, plus 1 gallon reserve

Rear wheels: 11x28 rear tires standard; tread adjustable from 56 to 84 inches in 4-inch steps

Front wheels: 5.5x16 4-ply front tires standard (dual tricycle)

Hydraulic system: enclosed hydraulics with Constant Draft Control and Implement Position Control; constant running, engine-driven vane type pump. (Remote cylinder unit optional)

Electrical system: 6-volt battery, two-brush
generator; volt and current regulator

Dashboard accessories: ammeter, oil pressure gauge,
temperature gauge, and Proof-Meter

Other regular equipment: muffler, fenders,
toolbox, adjustable top link (three-point
hitch), and drawbar stays

Overall Measurements
Wheelbase at 56-inch tread......85.3 inches
Maximum height.....................64.57 inches
Maximum length....................132.0 inches (700); 132.4
                                                    inches (900)
Maximum width at 84-inch tread 95.50 inches
Crop clearance ....27.2 inches (700); 27.9
                                                    inches (900)
Approximate weight ....3,100 pounds (700);
                                                    3,184 pounds.(900)
*Specifications and data obtained from operators manuals
and sales literature, 1955.*

Options and Accessories for 600-900 Tractors

•PTO pulley assembly used in either the left, right, or down position. The pulley assembly was introduced with the 9N tractor.

•ASAE PTO conversion assembly converted the Ford tractor to ASAE standards. The conversion kit included a safety shield, PTO extension, drawbar stay braces, and drawbar extension.

•The Selec-Trol Valve was used to direct the flow of hydraulic power from the hydraulic system to remote cylinders for operation of a variety of auxiliary equipment.

half cabs

FOR FORD AND FORDSON MAJOR DIESEL TRACTORS

Here's the last word in driver comfort and protection against the weather . . . Half Cabs for all model Ford and Fordson Major Diesel Tractors. These Half Cabs attach quickly. They offer such features as excellent operator vision, hinged doors on both sides for ease of getting on and off tractor, sturdy construction and removable motor flaps for those warm days. But that's not all . . . Half Cabs for Ford Tractors now have adjustable tilting windshields. This new windshield affords full protection in cold weather, yet it raises to provide ventilation for operator comfort when weather is warm.

These new Half Cabs are designed especially for Ford and Fordson Major Diesel Tractors . . . made of weather-proof canvas on a sturdy metal frame, they're built to fit . . . they're designed to take the cold out of tractor operation.

KIT NO. 231261 HALF CAB
for FORD MODELS 700 and 900
TRICYCLE TRACTORS

KIT NO. 231259 HALF CAB
for FORD MODELS 600, 800 and
NAA 4-Wheel Tractors

KIT NO. 231052 HALF CAB
for FORDSON MAJOR
DIESEL TRACTORS

KIT NO. 231260 HALF C
for FORD MODELS 9N, 2N
8N 4-Wheel Tractors

As with previous Ford model tractors, options like these half-cab kits were available for the 600-900 Series tractors as well. The cabs pictured above are made of canvas and mounted on a steel frame. Kits usually offered tilting windshields, engine flaps, rear curtains, and doors. *Ford Motor Company flyer, 1958*

•A grease gun and bracket was available for lubricating chores around the farm; the bracket could be mounted on the fender of the tractor.

•Remote control attachments were available that consisted of a control valve and remote control cylinders. These attachments were used for adjusting pull-type implements and also allowed one to do odd jobs around the farm with smaller hydraulic-driven tools.

•The stabilizer link kit was used to help eliminate "sway" during middlebusting operations. The stabilizer bars had no effect on the operations of the hydraulics or action of the tractor.

•Tire pump and gauge kit is flexible 16-foot hose that reached all four wheels of the tractor and could be used to air up just about anything around the farm. The pump was actuated by the use of engine compression; one spark plug was removed, and a brass hose connector was inserted. Engine idle was all you needed; a gauge was used to monitor air pressure.

•A cigarette lighter could be installed as a kit.

•Wheel weights could be purchased at extra cost. For rear wheels, 12 segmented weights could be placed individually or all at once, depending on the operator's needs. They included two mounting discs (68 pounds), 24 segments at 30 pounds each, and 12 pounds of bolts for a total of 800 pounds. Front weights were also available, consisting of a 130-pound box and six segments weighing 48 pounds each, a total of 418 pounds.

•Vertical exhaust kits were available for those who needed to keep the exhaust away from high crop work or where the conventional tailpipe could be damaged in rough working areas.

New FORD 601 SERIES
WORKMASTER TRACTORS

In 1958, Ford introduced its 601 to 901 tractors, offering both diesel and LP gas models in addition to the gasoline versions. Above is the Model 651 with five-speed transmission and transmission PTO. In all, there were eight different models within the 601 Series. The grilles on the 601 and 701 tractors were similar to the 600 to 900 Series tractors. The logo on the side of the hood was also followed by the model and "work" class. This tractor displays the optional Vari-Weights on the rear wheels. *Ford Brochure, 1959*

•An implement light kit consisted of a sealed-beam headlight (flood) with built-in switch, wiring, and mounting brackets.

•Dearborn Touch-Up enamel was available in gray, medium gray, and vermilion and could be applied with a brush or spray.

•Half-cabs were available from Ford as well other companies; all-weather cabs or full cabs could also be found.

•Power adjusted rear wheels were standard on the 900 Series and optional on others.

•The Rest-O-Ride tractor seat was standard on 800 Series all-purpose tractors.

•Dual rear-wheel kits were listed as an option for the 600 and 800 Series.

601 and 701 Series Profile

The powerplant offered with the 601 and 701 Series model tractors was essentially the same, outfitted with the standard 134-cubic-inch Red Tiger engine, while the diesel (operating with a 12-volt system) and LP gas engines were available as options. The Red Tiger engine featured freely rotating exhaust valves to maintain compression longer, aluminum pistons, a balanced crankshaft, and a fast-acting governor mounted on the crankshaft for instant response. It also featured a weatherproof ignition system, a fuel-saver carburetor delivering efficient fuel mixtures at varying speeds, and a pressurized oil system.

Systems dealing with electrical, cooling, and fuel were very similar. The model number in each series determined standard equipment. For instance, the Model 611 and 621 (the "bare bones") lacked the Proof-Meter, tools, lights, Rest-O-Ride seat, two-speed PTO, ground-driven PTO, and the hydraulic system with three-point hitch. Many of these features were optional, including power-adjusted rear wheels, power steering (standard on row croppers), and the one-speed (540 rpm) PTO. All models in the 601 and 701 Series, with the exception of the 611, 621, and 631, offered the following standard equipment: safety starter, key ignition, battery, generator, voltage and current regulator, oil pressure gauge, fuel gauge, generator warning light, thermostat, oil bath air cleaner, full flow oil filter, muffler, fenders, and temperature gauge. Only the Models 611 and 621 came without the hydraulic system and three-point linkage as standard equipment.

The row crop version of the 601 Series was the 701. Two models were available in this series, the 741 and the 771, and both models could be ordered with either dual

Above is the Model 641, equipped with the four-speed transmission and transmission PTO. Proof-Meter, tools and tool box, lights, and hydraulics with three-point linkage were standard equipment. *Ford Brochure, 1959*

front wheels, the wide adjustable front axle, or the single front wheel. The biggest differences between the two 701 Series models was the transmission and PTO. The 741 came with the four-speed transmission and transmission-driven PTO, while the 771 was equipped with the Select-O-Speed transmission for on-the-go shifting and the 540 rpm independent PTO. The Select-O-Speed featured 10 forward speeds and 1 reverse speed. Company literature claimed that one could shift from 10th to 4th gear, increasing drawbar pull by eight times. More often than not, Select-O-Speed transmissions didn't work quite the way they were supposed to, and in many cases were swapped for conventional four- or five-speed transmissions.

As with the earlier NAA model tractors, Constant Draft Control and Implement Position Control were offered on all models with the hydraulic system. Remote cylinders and other related accessories were optional.

801 and 901 Series Profile

The upper end of the Ford tractor line in 1958 was the 801 and 901 Series tractors. In addition to standard gasoline engines, in 1958 Ford introduced its diesel and LP gas packages. Both diesel and gasoline versions ran the 172-cubic-inch Red Tiger engine. The rated horsepower on the gas model was 45 but could be increased to 50 horsepower by increasing the size of the carburetor, manifold, air cleaner, and muffler. The 801-901 Series retained many of the features of the 800-900 Series tractors with respect to electrical, cooling, and other standard operating systems (the diesel version ran on a 12-volt system). All models in the 801-901 Series offered the Rest-O-Ride seat as standard with the exception of the Model 811 and 821. The Select-O-Speed transmission was offered on two additional models in the 801-901 Series, and power-adjusted wheels were standard only on the 901 Series row crop tractors. Below is a quick reference table, followed by serial numbers, specifications, and options.

601, 701, 801, and 901 Series/Model Reference Table*

601 Series All-Purpose Model Tractors

All models came with hydraulic system and three-point linkage, 11x28 4-ply rear tires, and wheel spacing from 52 to 76 inches.

641: four-speed with transmission PTO
651: five-speed with transmission PTO
661: five-speed with live PTO
671: Select-O-Speed with 540 rpm independent PTO
681: Select-O-Speed with two-speed (540 and 1,000 rpm) independent PTO and ground speed PTO

601 Special Utility Models

All models came with 10x28 4-ply rear tires with wheel spacings from 48 to 76 inches.

611: Select-O-Speed without PTO

621: four-speed, transmission PTO optional

631:-four-speed, transmission PTO optional, hydraulic system, and three-point linkage

701 Series Row Crop Model Tractors

Both models included power steering, Rest-O-Ride seat, choice of front ends, hydraulics with three-point hitch, and 11x28 4-ply rear tires with rear wheel spacings from 56 to 84 inches.

741: four-speed with transmission PTO

771: Select-O-Speed with 540 rpm independent PTO

801 Series All-Purpose Model Tractors

All models listed below came with hydraulics and three-point hitch, Rest-O-Ride seat, and 12x28 4-ply rear tires with wheels spacings from 52 to 76 inches.

841: four-speed with transmission PTO

851: five-speed with transmission PTO

861: five-speed with live PTO

871: Select-O-Speed with 540 rpm independent PTO

881: Select-O-Speed with two-speed (540 and 1,000 rpm) independent PTO and ground speed PTO

801 Series Special Utility Models

Both models listed in this series came with 10x28 four-ply rear tires with wheel spacings from 48 to 76 inches.

811: Select-O-Speed without PTO

821:four-speed, transmission PTO optional

901 Series Row Crop Model Tractors

All row crop models listed below included power steering, Rest-O-Ride seat, power-adjusted rear wheels, choice of front ends, hydraulics, and three-point linkage, 12x28 4-ply rear tires with spacings from 56 to 84 inches.

941: four-speed with transmission PTO

951: five-speed with transmission PTO

961: five-speed with live PTO

971: Select-O-Speed with 540 rpm independent PTO

981: Select-O-Speed with two-speed (540 and 1,000 rpm)

601 ALL-PURPOSE SERIES

These 4-wheel tractors are compact and maneuverable, and are available with both Select-O-Speed and conventional 4- and 5-speed transmissions. Also in fully equipped and in low-cost special utility models.

Industrial Front End: Heavy duty axle and heavier clutch, is a factory installed option.

The Model 681 was the top of the line in the 601 Series. Standard equipment was the Select-O-Speed (10 forward gears and 2 reverse); 2-speed 540 and 1000 rpm independent PTO and ground speed PTO. Again, styling is very similar to the earlier 600 Series tractors. The 601 Series could also be had with the 144 ci diesel engine (introduced in 1958) with the 12-volt electrical system. *Ford Brochure, 1959*

independent PTO and ground speed PTO

(All models were available with diesel engines; 144 ci for 601 and 701 Series; 172 ci for the 801 and 901 Series)

Data obtained from Workmaster Tractor literature, 1959.

Serial Numbers for 601, 701, 801, and 901 Tractors

1957 1001
1958 11977
1959 58312
1960 105943
1961 131427
1962 155531

Specifications for 601-701 Series (Workmaster) Tractors*

Engine: Red Tiger four-cylinder inline overhead

THE WORKMASTER SERIES

DUAL FRONT WHEELS

SINGLE FRONT WHEEL

WIDE ADJUSTABLE FRONT AXLE

701 ROW CROP SERIES

Available with your choice of front ends, this tractor is well suited for any kind of row crop work. Power steering is standard equipment. Four-speed and Select-O-Speed transmissions.

The 701 Series row crop models consisted of the 741 and 771. The 741 had the same power plant as the 601 models and was only available with a four-speed transmission with transmission PTO; power steering also became available as standard equipment on all Ford row crop tractors. The Model 771 offered Select-O-Speed with the 540 rpm independent PTO. Dual front wheels (tricycle-type) and the single front wheel was also available. Pictured below left is the 541 Off-Set, that was actually a redesigned 600 Series tractor, offering the same equipment as the Model 741. *Ford Brochure, 1959*

valve. Bore 3.44 inches, stroke 3.6 inches; 134 ci displacement; compression ratio 7.5 to 1. Idle speed 450 to 750 rpm; maximum governed speed (no load) 2,200 rpm; 43.0 brake horsepower without accessories at 2,000 rpm; at flywheel 117 foot-pounds of torque at 1,500 rpm, without accessories. The 144 ci Ford diesel engine was also available for the 601-901 Series after 1958. The compression ratio for the diesels was 16.8 to 1 and featured aluminum pistons, forged steel crankshaft and opposed plunge distributor injection pump, with the four-hole, long-stem open injectors. The LP gas models could be factory ordered and operated on butane, propane, or by a mixture of the two fuels.

Crankshaft: precision cast-alloy iron (forged steel on diesel).

Main bearing journal size

Front ....2.49-inch diameter by 1.49-inch length

Middle ....2.49-inch diameter by 1.75-inch length

Rear ....2.49-inch diameter by 1.64-inch length

Connecting rod journal size ....2.30-inch diameter by 1.25-inch length

Connecting rods: forged alloy steel

Pistons: Autothermic aluminum alloy-cam ground

Rings: 3/32-inch width top compression, chrome-plated; 3/32-inch width lower compression, phosphate-plated

Piston pin: full-floating, lubricated by continuous splash; 0.912-inch diameter by 2.84 inches in length

Piston travel: 1,200 feet per minute at 2,000 rpm

Valves, inserts, springs, and guides: overhead valves with removable cast-chromium-molybdenum-tungsten steel alloy exhaust inserts, steel coil springs, and replaceable valve guides

Lubrication: pressure type with full flow oil filter

Cooling system: tube and fin radiator with pressure cap. Three-blade curved tip fan 15.7 inches in diameter, pump capacity 16 gallons per minute at 1,400 engine rpm; thermostat fully open at 177 to 182 °F

Carburetor: single updraft plain tube type with dustproof construction and accelerating well. Marvel Schebler 1-inch SAE flange size; adjustable main jet.

Air cleaner: oil bath with removable lower element for cleaning; 8-pint capacity

Governor: centrifugal flyball, variable speed; enclosed mounted on crankshaft for instant response to varying loads

Electrical system: two-brush generator; automatic spark advance and side-mounted distributor; safety starter switch is regular equipment; 6-volt battery; diesel models operated with a 12-volt system

Clutch: (Models 621, 631, 641, and 651) single-plate foot-operated, 10 inches in diameter; (Model 661) double-plate 9-inch diameter, foot-operated for transmission and PTO

Transmission: (Models 621, 631, and 641) constant mesh four-speed; (Models 651 and 661) constant mesh five-speed. Optional auxiliary over-under transmission providing 12 forward speeds, 3 reverse speeds, and 3 PTO speeds for Models 621, 631, and 641. Select-O-Speed transmission was standard on Models 611, 671, 681, and 771

Steering: Recirculating ball-nut gear (Power steering offered as factory option)

Hydraulic system: Ford produced pump with six pistons; wobble plate actuated. Driven by helical gear off of camshaft gear. Flow is 4 gallons per minute at 2,000 engine rpm; operating pressure

2,000 psi maximum; relief valve pressure
2,000 rpm

Brakes: Internal expanding, self-energizing; 14-inch
double-anchored, both individually or jointly
operated with the right foot; also equipped
with locks

Rear wheels: (Models 621 and 631) standard 10x28
tires. Tread adjustments in 4-inch steps from
48 to 76 inches. (Models 641, 651, and
661) 11x28 standard tires with tread adjustment
from 52 to 76 inches in 4-inch steps;
(Models 741 and 771) 11x28 standard tires
with tread adjustments from 56 to 84
inches. The row crop models were available
with dual front wheels, adjustable front axle,
or single front wheel. High cleat or all
nonskid "button" tread available as
optional equipment.

Front wheels: (All models) 5.50x16 tires standard. Tread
adjustment from 52 to 80 inches. Front wheel
conversion allows the use of 6.00x16 tires
(optional) for heavy front-end work. Industrial
tread also available at extra cost.

Dimensions

Wheelbase at 52-inch ....74.50 inches
front tread
Overall height with ....56.93 inches
11-inch rear tires
Overall length at ....120.83 inches
52-inch front tread
Overall width at ....63.88 inches
52-inch tread
Overall width at ....87.50 inches
76-inch tread
Ground clearance......................13.22 inches

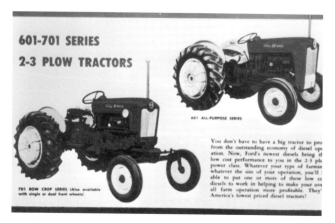

Similarities between the 601 and 701 Series models are shown here. Note the vertical exhaust on both models. *Brochure, 1958*

under transmission case
Clearance under rear axle ....21.19 inches
Approximate shipping weight..2,812 pounds
Working weight: tires ....4,716 pounds
filled, front and rear weights
Specifications and data obtained from Workmaster operators manuals and sales literature, 1959.

Specifications for 801 and 901 Series Tractors*

Engine: four-cylinder 172 ci Red Tiger engine; 45 horsepower (50 horsepower with larger manifold, carburetor, air cleaner, and muffler). Diesel also available with 16 to 1 compression ratio.

Lubrication: pressure type with full flow oil filter

Cooling system: tube and fin radiator with pressure cap. Three-blade curved-tip fan 15.7 inches in diameter; pump capacity 16 gallons per minute at 1,400 engine   rpm; thermostat fully open at 177 to 182 degrees

Carburetor: single updraft plain tube type with dustproof construction and accelerating well. Marvel Schebler 1-inch SAE flange size; adjustable main jet

Air cleaner: oil bath with removable lower element for cleaning, 8-pint capacity

Governor: centrifugal flyball, variable speed; enclosed mounted on crankshaft for instant response to varying loads

Electrical system: two-brush generator; automatic spark advance and side-mounted distributor; safety starter switch is regular equipment; 6-volt battery; diesel models operated with a 12-volt system

Clutch: single-plate foot-operated 10-inch diameter

Transmission: (Models 821 and 941) four-speed, with transmission PTO; (Model 821) four-speed with transmission PTO as an option; (Models 851 and 951) five-speed with transmission PTO; (Models 861 and 961) five-speed with live PTO; (Model 811) four-speed, PTO optional; (Models 871 and 971) Select-O-Speed with 540 rpm independent PTO; (Models 881 and 981) Select-O-Speed with 540 and 1,000 rpm independent PTO and ground-driven PTO. Optional auxiliary over-under transmission providing 12 forward gears and 3 reverse was also available.

Steering: recirculating ball-nut gear (Power steering offered as factory option)

Hydraulic system: Ford-produced pump with six

pistons; wobble plate actuated. Driven by helical gear off of camshaft gear. Flow is 4 gallons per minute at 2,000 engine rpm; operating pressure 2,000 psi maximum; relief valve pressure 2,000 rpm

Brakes: internal expanding, self-energizing. 14-inch double-anchored, both individually or jointly operated with the right foot; also equipped with locks

Rear wheels: (801 Series All-Purpose models) standard 12x28 tires. Rear tread adjustments in 4-inch steps from 52 to 76 inches. (801 Series Utility models 811 and 821) 10x28 standard tires with tread adjustment from 48 inches to 76 inches in 4-inch steps; (all 901 Series row croppers) 12x28 standard tires with tread adjustments from 56 to 84-inch. The row crop models were available with dual front wheels, adjustable front axle, or single front wheel. High cleat or all nonskid "button" tread available as optional equipment.

Front wheels: (all models) 5.50x16 tires standard. Tread adjustment from 52 to 80 inches. Front wheel conversion allows the use of 6.00x16 tires (optional) for heavy front-end work. Industrial tread also available at extra cost.

Specifications and data obtained from operators manuals and sales literature, 1958 and 1959.

Options and Accessories for 601-901 Tractors

•PTO pulley assembly used in either the left, right, or down position. The pulley assembly was introduced with the 9N tractor.

•ASAE PTO conversion assembly converts the Ford tractor to

ASAE standards. The conversion kit included a safety shield, PTO extension, drawbar stay braces, and drawbar extension.

•The Selec-Trol Valve was used to direct the flow of hydraulic power from the hydraulic system to remote cylinders for operation of a variety of auxiliary equipment.

•A grease gun and bracket was available for lubricating chores around the farm; the bracket could be mounted on the fender of the tractor.

•Remote control attachments were available that consisted of a control valve and remote control cylinders. These attachments were used for adjusting pull-type implements and also allowed one to do odd jobs around the farm with smaller hydraulic-driven tools.

•The stabilizer link kit was used to help eliminate "sway" during middlebusting operations. The stabilizer bars had no effect on the operations of the hydraulics or action of the tractor.

•The tire pump and gauge kit's flexible 16-foot hose reached all four wheels of the tractor and could be used to air up just about anything around the farm. The pump was actuated by the use of engine compression; one spark plug was removed and a brass hose connector was inserted. Engine idle was all you needed; a gauge was used to monitor air pressure.

•A cigarette lighter could be installed as a kit.

•Wheel weights could be purchased at extra cost. For rear wheels, twelve segmented weights could be placed individually or all at once, depending on the operator's needs. They included two mounting discs (68 pounds), 24 segments at 30 pounds each, and 12 pounds of bolts for a total of 800 pounds. Front weights were also available and consisted of a 130-pound box and six segments weighing 48 pounds each, a total of 418 pounds. (Rear heavy-duty weights were available for 800 Series tractors only.)

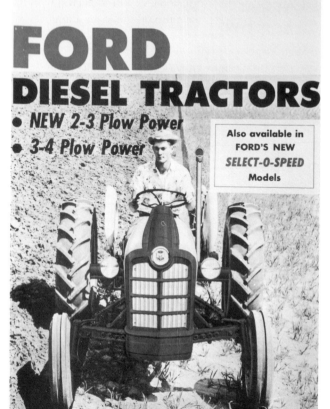

the lowest priced diesel tractors in their class

FORD
DIESEL TRACTORS

- **NEW 2-3 Plow Power**
- **3-4 Plow Power**

Also available in
FORD'S NEW
SELECT-O-SPEED
Models

Diesel power came to the Ford tractor line in 1958, and apparently was quite affordable compared to other manufacturers. The upper end of the series offered the 172 ci diesel with a compression ratio of 16.8 to 1. You will notice a grille change in the 801-901 Series as opposed to the 601-701 tractors. One vertical and three horizontal bars graced the front of the grille. *Brochure, 1959*

•Vertical exhaust kits were available for those who needed to keep the exhaust away from high crop work or where the conventional tailpipe could be damaged in rough working areas.

•An implement light kit was available and consisted of a sealed-beam headlight (flood) with built-in switch, wiring, and mounting brackets.

•Dearborn Touch-Up enamel was available in gray, medium gray, and vermilion and could be applied with a brush or spray.

•Half-cabs were available from Ford as well other companies; all-weather cabs or full cabs could also be found.

•A Rest-O-Ride seat was standard on 701, 801 All-Purpose, and 901 Series.

•Power steering was standard on 901 row crop models and was optional on others.

•Power-adjusted wheels were standard on 901 row crop models and optional on others.

Specifications for 501 Series
Off-Set Tractors
(Models 541 and 541-4)
(All off-set models came with the same standard features as the Model 741 row crop)
Engine: two types: 134 ci gasoline or LP gas with full-flow oil filter, 6-volt system, and voltage regulator; and 144 ci diesel with the 12-volt system

Transmission: four-speed constant mesh

Clutch: single disc, 10-inch

Hydraulics: piston pump with draft and position control; remote cylinder optional

PTO: transmission-driven, ASAE standard

Standard equipment: vertical exhaust; fuel, oil, and temperature gauges; proof-meter; lighting equipment, tools, and toolbox; and generator warning light. Also factory-installed "built-in-balance;" 325 additional pounds to the right rear axle

Dimensions
Model 541
Wheelbase ....89 inches
Overall length ....139.12 inches
Height to top of steering wheel70 inches
Turning radius...........................11 feet

Clearance
Under front axle ....25 inches
Under rear axle ....26.7 inches
Under belly ....19.5 inches
Weight......................................3,513 pounds

Tread adjustment
Front...40 to 86 inches
Rear..40 to 76 inches
(Maximum width requires 4-inch spacers on rear and reversing front wheels)

Model 541-4
Wheelbase ....89.55 inches
Overall length ....139.67 inches
Height to top of steering wheel76.32 inches
Turning radius...........................11 feet

Out of the 1959 sales brochure comes this ad for Select-O-Speed. Showing the positioning of the gear lever under the steering wheel, Select-O-Speed was touted as the best thing since sliced bread. With no clutching needed, the system was supposed to provide "on-the-go" shifting and overlapping speeds to increase power and efficiency. It also had the ability to run without interfering with the speed of the PTO. According to some, however, the Select-O-Speed found its way to the repair garage more often than not, being swapped out for conventional five-speed transmissions.

Clearance

Under front axle ....30 inches
Under rear axle ....31.7 inches
Under belly ....24.5 inches
Weight.....................................3,664 pounds

Tread adjustment

Front..40 to 86 inches
Rear..40 to 76 inches
(Maximum width requires 4-inch spacers on rear and reversing front wheels)

Sources/Selected Reading

Most of the information in this book was obtained from Ford tractor operators manuals/instruction books, sales literature (both original and reprinted versions), and phone interviews with several collectors of Ford tractors, from the Fordson to the 901 Series. Below is a list of sources used for general background and history of Ford tractor products.

Gray, R. B. Gray. *The Agricultural Tractor 1855-1950*. St. Joseph, Michigan: American Society of Agricultural Engineers, 1954.

Larson, Lester. *Farm Tractors 1950-1975*. St. Joseph, Michigan: American Society of Agricultural Engineers, 1981.

Leffingwell, Randy. *The American Farm Tractor*. Osceola, Wisconsin: Motorbooks International, 1991.

Pripps, Robert, and Andrew Morland. *Ford Tractors: N-Series, Ford and Ferguson 1914-1954*. Osceola, Wisconsin: Motorbooks International, 1990.

Rinaldi, Gerard, Ed. *9N-2N-8N Newsletter*. P.O. Box 235, Chelsea, Vermont 05038.

Appendix

Component Identification Numbers: 1939-1964

Generators
1939-1947	9N10000L
1947-1948	8N10000A
1948-1950	8N10000B
1950-1952	8N100001
(Ford Round)	
1953-1960	FAC 1000
& FAC 1000A	

Starters
1939-1952	11002 (Ford)
1963-1964	FAC 11001 P

Carburetors (Schebler)
1939-1952 TSX33 or TSX241
1953-1954 TSX428
1955-1957 TSX580 (600-700); TSX593 & TSX706 (800-900)
1958-1960 TSX652 (601-701); TSX813 (801-901)

Zenith #13876 used from 1939-1942

Decal Placement
1. 1939-1952: On top of oil filter cover, color: red/white/blue. Decal reads "Ford oil and motor cleaner."

2. 1939-1952: On side of oil cartridge, color: red/white/blue. Decal is "warning label."

3. 1939-1952: On side of air cleaner, color: blue/white. Decal reads "Important: for longer life service oil cup daily; very dusty conditions twice daily. Service body monthly."

4. 1947-on: Side of transmission housing by position control lever. Color: blue/white. Decal is diagram of position control operation.

5. 1952-on: Begining with the Jubilee model a "Be Careful" decal was placed on the backside of the differential housing and below the top link. The color was blue and white. Decal read "Pull only from standard drawbar or drawbar clevis. Do not hitch to axle or any point above."

Publications On Fordson/Ford Tractors
Ray Batchelor. *"Henry Ford: Mass Production, Modernism and Design,"* Manchester University Press, 1994.

Homer Jackson Dana. Collected Brochures: 1915-1950, no date.

Ford Motor Co. *Instruction Book for the Fordson Tractor: Agricultural, Industrial,* Golf Course, Land Utility and Row Crop, Ford Motor Co., 1946.

R.B. Gray. *The Agricultural Tractor 1855-1950* American Society of Agricultural Engineers, St. Joseph, MI, 1954.

Bruce M. Kneifl. *Ford Car, Truck and Tractor Restoration Directory,* Motorbooks International, 1992.

Lester Larson. *Farm Tractors 1950-1975* ASAE, St. Jopseph, MI, 1981

Randy Leffingwell. *The American Farm Tractor* Motorbooks International, Osceola, WI, 1991.

John B. Liljedahl. *Tractors and their Power Units,* Wiley Publications, 1979.

Robert Pripps and Andrew Morland. *Ford Tractors: N-Series, Ford and Ferguson 1914-1954,* Motorbooks International, Osceola, WI, 1990.

Robert Pripps. *Ford Tractors,* Motorbooks International, 1990.

Ford and Fordson Tractors, Motorbooks International, 1995.

Illustrated Ford and Fordson Tractor Buyers Guide, Motorbooks International, 1994.

Tractor Digest. *Tractor Digest,* Tytondale Publishers, 1994.

Michael Williams. *Ford and Fordson Tractors,* Blandford Press, 1985.

Virtually all Ford N-Series tractor shop manuals can be obtained from Ford-New Holland Publications at 20770 Westwood Dr., Strongsville, OH 44136. Toll free orders can be taken over the phone at 1-800-635-4913 or 216-572-7255.

Newsletters
9N-2N-8N Newsletter, Gerard Rinaldi, editor. PO Box 235 Chelsea, VT 05038.

Clubs
Ford/Fordson Collectors Assoc.
645 Loveland-Miamiville Rd.
Loveland Ohio 45140
Tel: (513) 683-4935
Jim Ferguson, Secretary

The Ford/Fordson Collectors Assoc. was established in 1992. The group consists of 14 regional directors and offers national registry for Ford tractors. The association has roughly 450 members and continues to grow with 15,000 Ford tractors (1917-1970) now registered. The regional director-members are listed below:

Palmer Fossum
10201 E 100th St
Northfield MN 55057

Phil Muritz
12622 Unger Rd
Smithburg MD 21783

Doug Norman
Rt 3 Box 141
Montevideo MN 56265

Dan Zilm
RR 1 Box 242
Clarmont MN 55824

Dwight Emstrom
Rt 2 Box 140
Galesburg ILL 61401

Dean Simmons
18320 Zolman Rd
Fredricktown OH 43019

Ron Stauffer
Rt 1 Box 233
Portland IN 47371

Duane Helman
Box 17
Rosewood OH 43070

Ira Stout
505 SCR 300 W.
North Vernon IN 47265

Bob Brown
Po Box 723
Newfield NJ 08344

Rufus Roberts
3845 Bradley-Brownlee Rd
Cortland OH 44410

Jack Crane
7645 E 200 N
Whitestown IN 46075

Floyd Rockwell
413 W Arlington Dr.
Trenton OH 45067

Dan Whalen
2277 Berry Rd
Amelie OH 45102

Metric Conversion

Original Unit	Multiplied By	Converts To
inches	2.54	centimeters
feet	30.48	centimeters
pounds	0.45	kilograms
gallons	3.79	liters
cubic inches	16.39	cubic centimeters
miles per hour	1.61	kilometers per hour
Fahrenheit temp.	9/5, add 32	Celsius temp.

INDEX